Introduction

James P. Cannon (1890–1974) was one of the outstanding leaders of American socialism. A member of the Industrial Workers of the World and the early Socialist Party, he was a founder of the Communist Party and of the American Trotskyist movement. He was national secretary of the Socialist Workers Party from its founding in 1938 until 1953. Thereafter, he was the party's national chairman and later national chairman emeritus until his death. He was elected to the International Executive Committee of the Fourth International at its founding conference in 1938.

The talk in the first section of this bulletin was given by Joseph Hansen in August 1975 as an educational feature of an SWP national convention at that time. It was first published in *International Socialist Review,* June 1979.

Joseph Hansen (1910–1979) was secretary to Leon Trotsky when the exiled Russian revolutionary leader was in Mexico. Hansen was a leader of the SWP and the Fourth International for many years. A number of his writings are being published posthumously by Pathfinder Press.

Hansen had intended to expand his talk for publication, incorporating material written by Cannon during the 1930s. Some of this material, annotated by George Breitman, is included as an appendix in this bulletin, where most of it is published for the first time.

JAMES P. CANNON THE INTERNATIONALIST

By Joseph Hansen

In considering James P. Cannon as an internationalist, it may prove useful to begin by eliminating some possible misunderstandings.

It is generally thought that by "internationalist" we mean someone who is interested in foreign causes. A good example in the recent past would be a person who sympathized with the Vietnamese and wanted them to win, or at least wanted them to be free to decide their own fate.

A current case is Angola where the country appears on the verge of civil war and where Portuguese imperialism is intervening in hope of eventually imposing a neocolonialist government.

The truth is many people can become keenly interested in developments in other countries, such as a famine, civil strife, a war, or commotion of some kind or another.

Their interest is good. It can become the first step in what might develop into true internationalism.

The big hurdle is *practice.* What do you propose to do about the issues that have aroused your interest, your sympathy or your anger?

Some people may think of turning to the United Nations. They think of the obligation of that body to do something. Others think of the U.S. government. They might even send a letter to their favorite congresswoman.

Such courses have at least one glaring defect. Dependence is placed on others doing something. It is a neat way to avoid becoming personally committed.

That kind of internationalism is quite different from the kind represented by Cannon. Internationalism as he saw it goes much beyond goodwill and good intentions. It must be placed within the framework of socialism.

Misunderstandings of internationalism

But even this is not sufficient. Still other misunderstandings are possible. In a revolutionary socialist grouping itself a wrong view can be taken of internationalism.

For instance, an internationalist is not necessarily a specialist in the sociology, economics, and politics of other countries. Thus, an American socialist who becomes an expert in Japanese affairs does not thereby automatically become an internationalist. An American socialist who devotes time and energy to the study of Japan may be able to write instructive articles on the subject. And such contributions may well be appreciated not only in the United States but in other countries, including Japan itself.

Since I am talking to an audience that is primarily American, the example may become more vivid if it is turned around. A Japanese socialist who concentrates on the American scene does not thereby automatically become an internationalist no matter how thorough his or her studies may be, or how much those studies may be appreciated even by Americans.

If it were possible to become an internationalist simply by choosing some foreign country, drawing up a reading list of material on it, and retiring to a library until the material is mastered, it would greatly simplify matters. Still better, a person could obviously become more and more internationalist over the years by repeating this procedure over and over again. The more countries you become expert in, the greater you are as an internationalist. This could be called the quantitative theory of internationalism.

Jim Cannon held rather decided opinions on this. He felt that it was a revolutionist's first duty to master the affairs of one's own country. Over the years he had seen too many instances of individuals, especially those with intellectual pretensions, who had shirked their first duty, covering up their dereliction by becoming pseudo-experts on the affairs of other countries. A young comrade who failed to become absorbed in the problems of the American revolution and who turned instead to the problems of revolutions in other countries always remained somewhat suspect in Jim's eyes.

Lest a new misunderstanding arise at this point, let me stress that Jim placed high value on accurate knowledge of developments in other countries, particularly revolutionary developments. He was keenly alert to anything that might affect the world revolution, which in his view always had a decisive bearing on the course of American revolutionists, ranging from the task of explaining the meaning of the developments to organizing solidarity actions and seeking to take advantage of openings that might appear in the United States because of events abroad.

Within this framework Cannon appreciated the analyses and conclusions of American revolutionists who became genuine experts in the affairs of other countries. It goes without saying that he paid still closer attention to the analyses and conclusions of revolutionists native to countries where the class struggle became especially sharp and had worldwide repercussions.

Let me turn to another possible misunderstanding.

An internationalist is not necessarily distinguished by a capacity to work out revolutionary programs, particularly on the tactical level, for the revolutionists of other countries.

For example, an American might attempt to sit down and write a forty-eight-point program for a group of revolutionists in Indonesia. If Jim Cannon were alive, he would do his utmost to squelch such presumption on the grounds that it did not evidence an internationalist attitude but just the contrary.

If the situation were reversed and we in the Socialist Workers Party received a communication from a group in some other country proposing adoption of a program they had worked out for application in the United States, we would examine it with interest. Our interest would center primarily on seeing how much they really knew about the situation in the United States and about the concrete problems facing our party. We would also probably think that the group that had sent the proposed program had not yet achieved a truly internationalist outlook.

Again, to avoid any new misunderstanding, these imaginary cases do not involve the question of comradely collaboration in working out programs. And they do not involve the question of comradely criticism in instances where programs or courses of action have been proved by events to have been wrong.

In considering James P. Cannon as an internationalist, it is important to remove these possible misunderstandings. If you do not dispose of them, you might be taken in by some of his detractors, who long ago reached the conclusion that Cannon was an "American provincial." They mean by that he was a good militant, but one who never achieved international stature, since he did not become a specialist in the affairs of a single country outside the United States and never tried to dictate programs to revolutionists in other countries.

From Rosedale to a world view

To understand Cannon's development as an internationalist and to appreciate the level he finally reached, it is necessary to go back to the beginning of his career as a revolutionary socialist.

He learned about socialism from his father and from reading such literature as the *Appeal to Reason.* He began distributing the *Appeal to Reason* in 1906 at the age of sixteen. He joined the Socialist Party in 1908; but did not commit himself to the movement until 1911 at the age of twenty-one.

As a youth in the small midwestern town of Rosedale, Kansas, he could accurately be described as an "American provincial" although he was unusual in his range of intellectual interests.

What changed him from being an "American provincial" to something different? He was changed by the international outlook that socialism opened up for him. The flat prairie horizon which had seemed wide enough when he was a boy, gave way to a view that circled the globe. Jim's rebellion against the limitations, the restrictions, and the injustices to be seen in America found a goal in the vision of a new society built on the cooperation of human beings of all lands and races and on the mobilization of all of humanity's creative forces on a world scale.

Consider for a moment what had happened in this individual instance. A young man reared in one of the most backward regions of the United States had gained an understanding of the basic tenets of the most advanced theory of society and its course of development—the most developed that science had to offer. The result was an unusual combination.

Jim himself regarded it as quite novel. Here was a Rosedale kid who really fit in with the pool-hall gang, yet he had come to understand how the society around him was bound together by an international economic system that was absolutely certain to give way to a socialist order. Most important of all, he himself could play a role in helping the process along. That was the practical side. This was where theory was converted into practice.

A pool-hall tough with an internationalist socialist outlook. To his last days, Jim thought of this combination as something of a miracle, although it was not really that strange. In fact, others not much different from him were also going through this process. And Jim was absolutely convinced that millions of young Americans would eventually go through a similar experience.

What is important in evaluating Jim from this angle is that while he never forgot his origin as an "American provincial," what dominated his conscious life from then on was the international outlook that had come to him as a great illuminating vision.

As I mentioned, Jim committed himself to the socialist cause in 1911, when he joined the Industrial Workers of the World. He decided to dedicate himself to doing everything in his power to advance the cause of the international socialist revolution in the United States. That was how you converted theory into practice; and that was why he joined the Industrial Workers of the World. The IWW devoted itself to acting in the class struggle, not just theorizing about it. Socialism would be won by advancing the class struggle, not by dropping pieces of paper in a ballot box. What they nowadays call, in some countries, the electoral farce.

The IWW proved to be an invaluable school. Thrown into strikes and other battles, Jim soon learned the role that good leadership plays in assuring victories or in cushioning defeats. His natural talents in this respect soon brought him to the attention of some of the top leaders of the IWW, particularly Vincent St. John,[1] and they taught him everything they could.

Thus, in a relatively short time, Jim became a battle-hardened veteran in the American class struggle, a practitioner of socialism in this preparatory stage, an expert in tactics and strategy. He was a representative of the continuity of leadership in this very rough and at times quite violent field. Jim counted his continuity going right back to Albert Parsons, a great American revolutionary leader and one of the Haymarket martyrs, who were hanged in 1887 because of their militant role as labor organizers.

Jim, it should be stressed, considered the battles he became involved in as simply part of the necessary preparation for the coming American revolution, which, in turn, was but part of the world revolution that would topple capitalism and make it possible to build socialism on an international scale.

Internationalism in World War I

Unfortunately, it proved impossible to win with this straightforward course, no matter how natural it appeared to be on the surface.

In 1914, for the first time in history, a world war broke out. Still worse, the international socialist movement, which had even anticipated the event and warned that it would be met with revolution, fell to pieces. The socialist parties on the two sides came out for defense of the fatherland, that is, in support of their own capitalist classes. For many socialists everything seemed lost. Even if socialist theory remained valid, it had broken down in practice.

In the United States, the right-wing leaders of the Socialist Party took the side of the Allies. When Woodrow Wilson, who had been reelected president on the slogan, "He kept us out of war," decided to join the bloody but profitable conflict

---

1. Vincent St. John (1873–1929) was one of the principal leaders of the IWW and was its general secretary from 1908–14. He became an opponent of the Communist Party after it was formed.

and sent the doughboys to die on foreign battlefields, the right-wing socialists climbed onto the bandwagon, where they made spectacles of themselves selling war bonds.

The left wing of the Socialist Party, to which Jim naturally belonged, was incapable of working out an effective line of opposition to the war. The best it could come up with was resistance to the draft. It was left up to the young men in the Socialist Party to declare themselves as conscientious objectors on an individual basis.

This line did not arouse Jim's enthusiasm. In fact, he found it distasteful. Nevertheless, because nothing better was proposed, he became a conscientious objector. Later he was to describe what a political blunder this course represented from the socialist point of view. Among other things, the party should have sought to place its members inside the armed forces where, day in and day out, they could have explained their opposition to the war to an audience that was bound to become more and more receptive to the message.

Jim's judgment in this is quite correct. Nonetheless it is worth noting that in applying this line, Jim's intent was clearly internationalist. Conscientious objection, while ineffective, represented opposition to imperialist war—opposition, moreover, to his own ruling class and its government during the war itself.

Russian revolution intervenes

Before 1917, like other militants in the left wing of the Socialist Party who were becoming known for their leadership capacities, Jim puzzled over what had happened to the socialist movement because of the war. Without really being aware of it, he was moving toward the question of the politics of the socialist movement.

The Russian revolution, culminating in the triumph of the Bolsheviks in November 1917, altered the entire situation. The debacle in the international socialist movement caused by the betrayals of the parties belonging to the Second International appeared to have been overcome at one stroke. The world revolution had scored a decisive advance. For the first time since the Paris Commune in 1871, revolutionary socialists had won governmental power. They had proved in practice the validity of socialist theory.

Today, almost sixty years after that great event, it is difficult to visualize the enthusiasm it created among the masses on a world scale including inside the United States. Here it opened up a completely new perspective. Figures like Cannon responded as if they had been given a new lease on life. They set themselves two main tasks. First, to support the Bolsheviks with every means at their command. Second, to learn how the Bolsheviks achieved their victory so as to be able to apply those lessons to the United States.

This work proceeded along factional lines inside the Socialist Party. The adherents of the Bolsheviks set out to organize a movement capable of applying the methods of the Russians in the United States. They did this even while they studied everything they could obtain elucidating those methods. This material was not abundant because of the language problem and the conditions of the times. Consequently gaps in knowledge, ill-digested concepts, and outright misunderstandings were rather widespread.

Nevertheless, in responding to the formation of the Communist International in 1919, the left wing split from the Socialist Party and set out to apply in the United States what they thought they had learned from the experience of the Russian revolution. The split was a ragged one, ending in the formation of public factions that designated themselves as parties.

Matters were made more complicated by a witch-hunt that was, if anything, more ferocious than the one that took place in the 1950s under Senator McCarthy, and the fledgling American Communists of those days had little choice but to go underground.

Birth of American Bolshevism

In the spring of 1920, when two of the factions joined together to form the United Communist Party, Cannon was elected to the Central Committee and assigned to the St. Louis-Southern Illinois district of the party. A few months later he was sent to Cleveland to edit the *Toiler,* and a couple of months after that he was called to New York to serve as a resident member of the Central Committee. From then on he was in the central leadership.

The recognition of Cannon as a leader of national stature did not come as a result of any contributions on the theoretical or philosophical level. It came because of his intimate knowledge of the labor movement and his ability as an organizer. A top-rate politician of that kind was precisely what the center needed.

The main lesson that Cannon had drawn from the Russian revolution was the need for a party of the kind Lenin had built. In the immense task of carrying forward the American revolution, Cannon had reached the conclusion that the key to success lay in constructing a party on the Leninist model. He contrasted that, of course, in his mind with the experience under the Wobblies, who had no such party, and with the experience in the Socialist Party, which was not a Leninist party.

You could say that a new level had been reached in the extraordinary combination of qualities now to be found in James P. Cannon. In him was embodied the very best in the American socialist tradition, not merely in the form of knowledge gained from reading but in the form of living experience in the class struggle itself. This rich experience and consciousness of its continuity with the past struggles of the working class in America had now become fused with Bolshevism, the very latest development in international Marxism.

It is true that at this stage Jim's Bolshevism was still rough hewn. But he knew that Bolshevism represented a qualitative advance in carrying out the task of proceeding from the theory of socialism to its successful application in a revolution. He had dedicated his life to precisely that objective, and so he set out to become adept in Bolshevism. Jim's approach was that of a true internationalist. He wanted to put the ideas of the Bolsheviks into practice, right at home, in his own land, where he was born and raised. It was because of what it could mean in practice that he became a student of the Russians; that is, of the Russians of 1917.

Jim could be described at that point as a revolutionist of action, a prototype of those whom Trotsky expected to come more and more to the fore as the fulfillers of what Marx and Engels had forecast in theory.

As one of the founding leaders of the Communist Party, Jim acted as he had previously and as he was to act to the last day of his life. He tried to size up the situation faced by the party and to work out solutions or possible solutions to the problems that had to be met if the party were to move forward. And, of course, to move forward meant moving within the framework of the basic principles of revolutionary Marxism.

The early factionalism

The next three years—from 1920 to 1923—were very important in Cannon's development as an internationalist.

The American Communist Party consisted of various factions, tendencies, and cliques, each with its own prescriptions as to what to do in relation to the issues of the day. As a whole their proposed lines were ultraleftist, sectarian, doctrinaire, and dogmatic. The majority of the membership consisted of foreign-born workers, who tended to follow events through publications in their own language, and who considered themselves to stand at a higher cultural level than American-born workers, an estimate that was generally true.

How were such disparate groupings to be developed into a politically homogeneous party and brought into effective connection with the American class struggle? Cannon saw the problem clearer than anyone, and he worked away at trying to solve it.

One of the big difficulties was that an authoritative central leadership had not yet been established. The party remained divided in warring factions, a reflection of the fact that a politically homogeneous leadership team had not yet emerged. The leaders of the factions were engaged in a struggle to assert themselves and to establish their authority.

The task was to bring out the political issues and to subject the various lines of the factions to the test of events. This, of course, had to be done in relation to the concrete situation inside the United States.

Cannon participated vigorously in this struggle for leadership and in the process gained additional skill as a faction fighter. In fact, throughout the party his generalship in these battles was considered to be of the highest caliber.

This rough-and-tumble training in leadership, though one-sided, was very important. Still more important, however, was the attitude displayed by the leadership of the Communist International under Lenin and Trotsky.

First of all, the Communist International in those

days had no ulterior motives. Lenin and Trotsky did not favor this or that grouping because of the needs, or supposed needs, of the Kremlin's foreign policy, or to strengthen a faction inside Russia.

Second, when appeals were made to their judgment, they listened carefully to both sides or if there were three sides, they listened to all three. They operated fairly and loyally. Their reputation was such that all sides in a dispute counted on them to act with complete honesty. They took time in their deliberations, refusing to move hastily. They were objective. They did not try to settle old scores or defend previous errors.

Third, they tended to let the fight continue its natural course, viewing it as a normal process through which a young party develops a leadership capable of standing on its own feet. When they thought the time had come to express an opinion, they relied on careful explanation.

Fourth, they were completely open to argument and were ready to change their opinions if they felt that the arguments were persuasive.

Fifth, they relied heavily on advice and refrained from organizational crackdowns.

The result was that the Communist International played a highly positive role in helping the young party to find its way through the difficulties that beset it. The Comintern genuinely sought to do everything in its power to place its knowledge and experience at the disposal of the leadership of the American party as a whole, so as to help it to the maximum in developing a competent revolutionary leadership.

The attitude of the Communist International thus provided Cannon with a model of how an international center should operate. The model was not a facsimile but the original, so to speak. The Comintern had immense authority. Behind it stood the Bolsheviks under the leadership of Lenin and Trotsky. Moreover, the Comintern had huge resources, being backed by a state power. Yet there was no cracking of the whip. The Comintern proceeded reasonably, with a comradely attitude, seeking collaboration, and functioning in a collaborative way. And there could be no doubt that that was the way Lenin and Trotsky wanted it. They insisted on the Comintern using its authority judiciously and in strict relationship to the realities facing the national sections. That was the quickest, easiest, and soundest way to build an international of revolutionary parties, led by national leaderships that could do the job.

As was only natural, this model sank into Jim's mind. In the position of a leader of a national section, he directly experienced how leaders of the caliber of Lenin and Trotsky proceeded in trying to help construct a national leadership capable of leading a revolution.

It should be noted that Jim's primary orientation remained that of taking what he learned from the Bolsheviks and applying it to the American scene; that is, specifically, putting into practice the Bolshevik method of building a party of revolutionary cadres.

Changing role of the Comintern

The next period, from 1924 to 1928, constituted a completely unexpected chapter in Jim's development as a party leader and internationalist.

The objective difficulties facing the party in the United States became intense in face of a big boom in the economy and a resulting sag in the class struggle. In this situation, what was required was consolidation of the party leadership and preparation of the ranks for the economic depression that would inevitably end the boom. That would put the party in the best possible position to advance with giant strides.

However, all kinds of new obstacles kept blocking a favorable outcome to the struggle of contending factions in the party. In fact the struggle worsened and began taking ugly and dangerous forms. The role of the Comintern became increasingly suspect. For instance, the faction headed by Cannon and Foster[2] succeeded in gaining a majority at the Fourth Convention of the party in 1925 only to see the Comintern intervene, cancel it out, and put a minority in charge of the party.

Lenin had died in 1924. The faction struggle that he had initiated against Stalin and the bureaucratism that Stalin represented was carried on by Trotsky. But that origin of the struggle was not known abroad. The issues themselves were ill

2. William Z. Foster (1881–1961) joined the CP in 1921 after having achieved renown as an organizer of the national steel strike of 1919. He was the CP's candidate for president in 1924, 1928, and 1932, and was party chairman after World War II.

understood by the American Communist Party leaders, particularly in view of the fact that the documents of the Left Opposition organized by Trotsky were not made available. The Stalinist faction drove savagely to crush the opposition, and it used the Comintern to advance that objective on an international scale.

The Left Opposition mounted a heroic political struggle against the mounting reaction forming around Stalin. The political stands they took proved to be correct in every instance. But the full import of the struggle was not grasped at that time even by Trotsky. Trotsky did not reach a rounded assessment of the development of Stalinism until after the debacle in Germany in 1933, when Hitler took power without the German Communist Party putting up any serious struggle at all.

Trotsky presented his final, rounded theoretical conclusions in an article dated February 1, 1935, entitled "The Workers State, Thermidor and Bonapartism," which is an article I highly recommend, and in his book *The Revolution Betrayed,* which he completed in August 1936 and which was published in 1937.

The American Communist cadres, like most of those outside of the Soviet Union, were unable to see the international significance of the struggle. From afar, in the absence of adequate information, it looked like an obscure factional struggle over domestic issues in the Soviet Union. Perhaps at bottom it was only a power struggle inside the Russian party.

Thus the perspective appeared obscure and disheartening, and—while things were not as bad as in the period from 1914 to 1917 during the world war—the world revolution, including its American sector, was not moving ahead. In fact, it seemed to be falling back. Something was decidedly wrong in practice.

Defending Leninism against Stalinism

For Cannon, this period ended in the summer of 1928 when as a delegate to the Sixth Congress of the Communist International he accidentally received a copy of an important document written by Trotsky, then in exile in Alma Ata. The document was *The Draft Program of the Communist International: A Criticism of Fundamentals.* [Printed in *The Third International After Lenin,* Pathfinder Press, 1974.]

This document clarified the issues for Cannon. He became completely convinced of the correctness of Trotsky's views. The conviction was all the more impelling because of the insights it offered into what had been happening in the American section during the previous four years.

Cannon himself explained his reactions many times. In view of the fact that his motives are still being questioned in some quarters, I think he is entitled to take the floor. Listen to his words in the introduction to *The First Ten Years of American Communism:*

> The degeneration of the Communist Party did not swallow up everybody in its ranks. A small minority revolted against Stalinism without capitulating to American imperialism. There were reasons for that too.
>
> Those gossips who explain the degeneration of the majority as the natural result of their personal traits and delinquencies, or as the logical outcome of immoral communism, are puzzled by this apparent deviation from the rule. They are at a loss to explain why a few of the original communists became neither Stalinist flunkeys nor government informers, but remained what they had been and continued the struggle for the revolutionary program under the leadership of Trotsky and the Russian Opposition.
>
> The moralistic judges have been especially puzzled by the circumstance that I was among them; was, in fact, the initiator; and—still more inexplicably—have held consistently to that position in 25 years of struggle. These noble commentators on the doings and motivations of others never fail to point out that I was mixed up in all the factional alley-fights of the party, without any pretensions to nonpartisan holiness, then or afterward, and that I have neglected to offer any apologies or make any confessions—and on this point they do not lie. How then, they ask, could such a person "come out for Trotsky" after he was completely defeated, expelled, and isolated in exile in far away Alma Ata?
>
> That question has really intrigued the kibitzers, and there has been no lack of speculation as to the causes for my action. In my read-

ing of the political tradepapers, which is part of my routine, I have seen my revolt against the Stalinized Comintern in 1928 variously described as a "mistake," an "accident" and a "mystery"—the mistake, accident or mystery being why a communist faction fighter of the Twenties who, like all the others, fought to win, should deliberately align himself with a "lost cause"—and stick to it.

There was no mystery about it, and it was neither an accident nor a mistake. In the first chapters of my *History of American Trotskyism,* I have already told the truth about the circumstances surrounding my action in 1928 and the reasons for it. These reasons seemed to me to be correct and logical at the time as the simple duty of a communist—which I was, and am—and 25 years of reflection, combined with unceasing struggle to implement my decision, have not changed my opinion.

When I read Trotsky's "Criticism of the Draft Program" at the Sixth Congress of the Comintern in 1928, I was convinced at once—and for good—that the theory of "Socialism in One Country" was basically anti-revolutionary and that Trotsky and the Russian Opposition represented the true program of the revolution—the original Marxist program. What else could I do but support them? And what difference did it make that they were a small minority, defeated, expelled and exiled? It was a question of principle. This may be Greek to the philistine, but it is not an "accident" for a communist to act on principle, once it becomes clear to him. It is a matter of course.

My decision to support Trotsky and the Left Opposition in 1928, and to break with all the factions in the Communist Party over that issue, was not a sudden "conversion" on my part; and neither was my earlier decision in 1917 to support the Russian Revolution and the Bolsheviks and to leave the IWW behind.

Each time I remained what I had started out to be in my youth—a revolutionist against capitalism. The Russian Revolution and the Bolsheviks in the first instance, and the heroic struggle of the Left Opposition in the second, taught me some things I hadn't known before and hadn't been able to figure out for myself. They made me a better and more effective fighter for my own cause. But they did not basically change me into something I hadn't been before. They did not "convert" me to the revolution; I was a revolutionist to start with.

By way of further explanation, it should be pointed out that Jim understood to perfection what the immediate practical consequences of his espousal of the program of the Left Opposition would be. It meant expulsion from the party forthwith. It meant breaking relations with comrades with whom he had marched since 1919 and even before. It meant isolation. It meant being placed in the status of a pariah against whom everyone's blows were directed. It meant that years of practical party-building work went down the drain.

Jim consciously accepted all that because it was a matter of principle. He had to remain true to the cause to which he had dedicated his life in 1911.

In Cannon's development as an internationalist, the commitment to the Left Opposition in 1928 represented a qualitative step forward.

Role of the American revolution

He had become a leader of international importance in the struggle to cleanse the Comintern of the Stalinist filth and to restore the exemplary procedures of its first years under Lenin and Trotsky.

At the same time, he did not lose sight of the need to create a strong American base for the International Left Opposition. In this demanding task, he had full need for everything he had learned in the class struggle and in the factional battles in the left wing of the Socialist Party and in the formative stage of the Communist Party.

He needed above all, a correct concept of the role the American revolution is destined to play in ending the era of capitalism and opening the new era of a worldwide socialist society.

Trotsky's views on this are well-known. In his autobiography, he states that ever since his brief stay in New York in 1917, "the problem of 'America versus Europe' has been one of my chief interests. And even now [i.e., in 1929], I am studying the question with the utmost care, hoping to devote a separate book to it. If one is to understand the future destiny of humanity, this is the most important of all subjects." [Leon Trotsky, *My Life* (New York: Pathfinder Press, 1970), p. 372 (2014 printing).]

In noting his departure from the United States on March 27, 1917, Trotsky adds the following to his autobiography: "The Russian revolution came so soon that I only managed to catch the general life-rhythm of the monster known as New York. I was leaving for Europe, with the feeling of a man who had had only a peep into the foundry in which the fate of man is to be forged." [Ibid., p. 381.]

Following his exile from the Soviet Union in 1929, Trotsky reaffirmed this view in his first letter to the American Communists who had rallied to the Left Opposition.

Cannon referred many times to that letter. A good example can be found in his concluding speech to the May 31, 1953, meeting of the National Committee of the Socialist Workers Party. Here is what Cannon said:

> The most important party in the entire world is the Socialist Workers Party. It is the party with the greatest historical mission ever given to a group of people on this planet. Trotsky wrote in 1929, in his first letter to the founding group of our movement, that in the final analysis all the problems of this epoch will be solved on American soil; that, although in order of precedence it seemed that the revolution would come sooner in other countries than in the United States, a change in the historical order was easily possible which might put America in the first rank; and that in any case, a social crisis could arise in this country much sooner than anyone assumed, and from the beginning have a very feverish development. And Trotsky said that the conclusion from this perspective is that *it is necessary to prepare.* From that point of view, he said, our founding conference [May 1929], which he was addressing, had a world historic importance. [James P. Cannon, *Speeches to the Party* (Pathfinder, 1973), p. 186 (2009 printing). Emphasis in original.]

Cannon's insistence on this point has too often been misconstrued. It has been interpreted by some of his opponents and detractors as confirming that he was at bottom an "American provincial." Some have even interpreted it as a variety of chauvinism; that is, that Cannon was making an invidious comparison between the Socialist Workers Party and other sectors of the world Trotskyist movement. According to this interpretation, Cannon was expressing an arrogant attitude reflecting the pressure of American imperialism.

Such an interpretation is a gross error that only brings discredit on those who advance it. Cannon's point was completely internationalist. He was simply saying that the Russians had the honor of achieving the first big victory in the world revolution; but the honor of achieving the final victory in the world revolution will belong to the Americans. Nothing is settled in the world revolution until that final battle is won. From that elementary proposition, Cannon insisted on the decisive importance of the work of the Socialist Workers Party. Cannon stressed the responsibility that falls on the cadres of the American Trotskyist movement. But it also follows from this view that the healthy development of American Trotskyism is of prime importance to the international Trotskyist movement as a whole.

Others can quarrel with this view, but it should be understood that the quarrel ultimately is with Trotsky.

Cannon and Trotsky

The next eleven years, from 1929 to 1940, marked a fruitful period in the development of Cannon as an internationalist. For he now worked as a close collaborator with Trotsky in conducting the international struggle against Stalinism and in recruiting cadres in all parts of the world. I do not want to give the impression that Trotsky and Cannon represented a duumvirate, that is, a ruling coalition of two persons, for that was not at all the case. Leaders in various countries participated in this work on an equal footing, and Cannon was one of them.

The objective was to form a cohesive team of collaborators on an international scale, a team characterized by both its independence of thought and its capacity to pull together. Nonetheless, the brunt of much of the work fell to the Americans. That was because in those days, weak as the American contingent was, it was stronger than the other contingents.

A concrete example will indicate what I am referring to.

The main responsibility was given to the Americans to assemble the Commission of Inquiry into the Charges Made Against Leon Trotsky in the Moscow Trials; that is, the commission headed by John Dewey. The Dewey Commission went to Mexico, where Trotsky was then in exile, cross-examined him, asked for and received from him a great number of documents from his archives, and thoroughly examined the claims made by the prosecution in the trials that were staged in Moscow.

The commission was constituted on an international basis, and the Trotskyists in various countries, particularly France, helped facilitate its work. But the chief figure in the commission was John Dewey, an American educator and philosopher. And the main person on the organizational side was George Novack, an American who had graduated from the philosophical school taught by Dewey and had become a dialectical materialist and Trotskyist.

The commission found Trotsky not guilty, which made headlines in all the international papers. That verdict meant the end of Stalin's moral authority among the thinking public in the entire world. It constituted the most serious blow dealt to Stalinism prior to the Khrushchev revelations and the Hungarian revolution.

The outstanding achievement of that decade of close collaboration with Trotsky was, of course, the formation of the Fourth International in 1938. Here again Cannon played a key role in the preparatory work, particularly in organizing the struggle against those who disagreed with forming a Fourth International or who wanted to postpone it until some distant time in the future. Isaac Deutscher [the historian and biographer of Trotsky] was one of those in that category.

I was in Coyoacán during the discussions preceding the founding congress, and I recall Trotsky's asking Cannon to go to England in order to convince the comrades there to join together in a single organization that would select the British delegates to the founding congress. Trotsky was somewhat hesitant to ask Cannon to do this because of Cannon's age—he was forty-eight; and Trotsky thought that this running around should be done by a young person like Shachtman,[3] who was in his thirties. However, Trotsky was not sure that Shachtman would be as convincing as Cannon.

Cannon agreed to take the assignment and spent two weeks in England in the summer of 1938 before going on to France, where the founding congress was held. As the result of the work of an international delegation that he headed, three of the four groups he met with held a conference and established a unified section of the International, which was recognized by the founding congress.

For security reasons much of the work of the founding congress had to be done or prepared by special commissions that met in the weeks prior to the one-day congress. Cannon played a leading role in several of these commissions, including those that dealt with the internal problems of the French, Greek, and Mexican sections and the task of organizing defense and relief for revolutionists suffering persecution by the imperialists and the Stalinists. At the end of the congress he was elected to a fifteen-member International Executive Committee, and a week or two later, when reports about the congress began to reach Mexico, Trotsky wrote to Cannon's comrade and companion Rose Karsner,[4] "I regret very much that we don't have a couple of Jims more. At least one for Europe."[5]

---

3. Max Shachtman (1903–1972), a founder of the American Communist Party, was one of the first to join Cannon in defending Trotsky's views. He opposed defense of the Soviet Union in the 1939 war with Finland and split from the Socialist Workers Party to form the Workers Party, later the Independent Socialist League. At his death he was a leading figure in the right wing of the Socialist Party.

4. Rose Karsner (1889–1968) was a founder of the American Communist Party, the Communist League of America, and the Socialist Workers Party. She was Cannon's close political collaborator and companion from 1924.

5. In April 1938, shortly after extended discussion with Cannon in Mexico, Trotsky wrote a British comrade who had made an uncomplimentary remark about Cannon: "Cannon is the truest proletarian revolutionary in our movement. His quality is that he approaches every question from the point of view of its influence or importance for the unification of revolutionary workers. And it is especially this approach which shocks and astonishes petty-bourgeois intellectuals and dilettantes. In every important controversy Cannon was right."

The post-war split

With the assassination of Trotsky in August of 1940, the newly founded Fourth International was considered by many observers to be doomed. Among those holding this view was certainly the murderer in the Kremlin, who had acted in the belief that you can destroy the ideas of a genius by driving a pickaxe into his brain.

No one in the Fourth International, least of all James P. Cannon, had any illusions concerning the difficulties that now faced us. The opening battles of the Second World War were already being fought, and it was clear that the Soviet Union itself stood in deadly peril from the German military machine.

The intransigent opposition of the Socialist Workers Party to the new imperialist conflict meant that it could become the object of severe repressive blows, and this was soon to occur in the infamous Minneapolis trial that led to the imprisonment of the central leaders of the SWP, including Cannon.

In Europe, the cadres that had been assembled in the Fourth International suffered terrible blows. Many of them perished in the concentration camps or before firing squads.

Yet the Fourth International survived all the attempts to destroy it. Despite all the enormous pressures, its banner remained spotless. Not a single section violated the principles on which the movement was founded.

Following the war, new militants began to assume leadership responsibilities. This was particularly true in Europe; and it became a practical possibility to establish a new center there.

Cannon welcomed this development. In fact he considered it noteworthy evidence of the viability of the ideas and program of Trotskyism. In the turbulent situations then developing in Europe, he was of the opinion that openings for the Fourth International would appear on all sides, and that an energetic center was needed to take advantage of them.

All the sectors of the world Trotskyist movement, as he saw it, were duty bound to give full support to the new team. Naturally in Jim's book that meant that the American Trotskyists had to strive to be models in this respect.

This fruitful collaboration lasted until 1953. In that year, a painful factional struggle broke out on an international scale. Two factions formed. One was led by the International Secretariat under Pablo.[6] The other was led by the International Committee, James P. Cannon being the leading figure among the supporters of that group.

The differences appeared on several levels. On the organizational plane, various incidents had occurred that indicated a tendency on the part of the International Secretariat to operate in a way different from that practiced under Trotsky's guidance.

For instance, in France they intervened in the section and overturned a majority. In the United States, they intervened in a factional struggle without consulting the leadership of the party, thereby greatly exacerbating the struggle and turning it toward an outcome that was much more damaging than need have been.

On the political level, the International Secretariat went quite wrong in its general political prognosis, holding that the outbreak of World War III was imminent. From this followed a number of conclusions that proved to be disorienting.

This was coupled on the theoretical level by a view put forward by Pablo that for several centuries to come nothing better can be hoped for than workers states deformed at birth; that is, resembling the Soviet Union under Stalin.

In the course of that struggle, Cannon made some contributions that are worth studying on the problems of leadership both on the international level and on the level of national parties. In the following quotation, for instance, he explains his attitude toward the new international leadership that developed in Europe following World War II:

> Our relations with the leadership in Europe at that time were relations of the closest collaboration and support. There was general agreement between us. These were unknown men in our party. Nobody had ever heard of them.

---

6. Michel Pablo (1911–), whose real name is Raptis, was a Greek Trotskyist who became secretary of the Fourth International after World War II. During the split he was secretary of the International Secretariat faction until his arrest for aiding the Algerian revolution in 1960. Pablo participated in the reunification of the Fourth International in 1963, but split in 1965.

We helped to publicize the individual leaders, we commended them to our party members, and helped to build up their prestige. We did this, first because we had general agreement, and second because we realized they needed our support. They had yet to gain authority, not only here but throughout the world. And the fact that the SWP supported them up and down the line greatly reinforced their position and helped them to do their great work.

We went so far as to soft-pedal a lot of our differences with them—and I will mention here tonight some of the many differences, known for the most part only in our leading circles, that we have had in the course of the last seven years.

One difference was a tendency on their part toward "Cominternism" in organization matters—a tendency to set up the International as a highly centralized body on the order of the early Comintern, which could make decisions, enforce orders, and so forth in the old Comintern fashion. We said to them all the time, *"You can't do that.* The International is too weak, you are too weak. You can't have that kind of an International under present conditions. If you try it, you will only end up in weakening your own authority and creating disruption."

The old Comintern of Lenin's time had the concept of a highly centralized international organization from the first days, but there was a reason for it then. The reason was that there had been a revolution in Russia, and the whole world movement of socialism was reacting to it. The leaders of the Russian Revolution had an absolutely *decisive* moral and political authority. There were Lenin and Trotsky and Zinoviev and Radek and Bukharin—new great names that the revolutionary workers of the world were recognizing as the authentic leaders of the revolution. These were the men who set up, with the aid of a few others, the Comintern, the Third International.

They had state power in their hands. They had unlimited funds, which they poured out generously to subsidize and support the foreign parties. When there was a difference of opinion in any party, with two or three factions growing up, they could subsidize delegations to travel from any part of the world to Moscow. The differing groups could have full representation before the executive body to discuss the issues. The international leaders could get a real picture on the spot, hearing the representatives of the different tendencies themselves, before offering advice. And that's what they mainly offered in the early days—advice, and very few orders.

Speaking of representation, I was a delegate to Moscow five times. And every time I was there, delegates from other factions in the American CP were also there. At the Sixth Congress in 1928, we had about twenty delegates from the U.S., representing all three factions, and the whole expense was paid by the Comintern.

After the degeneration of the Russian party and the emergence of Stalinism, the centralism of the Comintern—which Trotsky and Lenin had handled like a two-edged sword, which they didn't want to swing carelessly—became in the hands of Stalin an instrument for suppressing all independent thought throughout the movement.

Instructed by the past experience, we understood the dangers for the present international movement. We believed it would be absolutely wrong to try to imitate a highly centralized international organization when we were so weak, when the ability to send delegates from different parties for common consultation was so limited, and when we could communicate only by correspondence. Under these conditions, we believed it would be better for the center there to limit itself primarily to the role of ideological leader, and to leave aside organizational interference as much as possible, especially outside of Europe.

In Europe, where the parties are close at hand, it might be organized a little more tightly. But even there, we had misgivings. Comrades who were there several times had misgivings about the tendency toward organizational centralization and discipline, even as applied to the different national parties close at hand in Europe.

That's one difference we had—a sort of run-

> ning, smoldering difference. We did not press our criticisms to the very end, although we had many. [*Speeches to the Party,* cited above, pp. 82–5.]
>
> Now one final word about internationalism. Internationalism will be useful for our party if it has a unifying effect and it will not be useful if it promotes a split or if it encourages a split in any way. Internationalism in our book means international collaboration. International collaboration to work out common ideas and to build up the parties and the leadership. But internationalism doesn't mean—I just want to make this clear as the final point—that leaderships in a national party can be made up or taken apart on order, that they can be removed by mechanical means or that they can be appointed.
>
> I say a party that cannot select its own leaders is not worth a cent. A party that will permit its leadership to be imposed by any other way except the clear will of its own membership can be as internationalist as it wants to but it wouldn't be worth anything to the International. The real problem of our party, everywhere throughout the world, is to throw up indigenous leaders who have the confidence and support of their own rank and file. I believe we've got that now, at least in the majority—in the decisive majority—and I think this majority is strong enough to lead the party and make it possible for people of different opinions to live within the framework of those conditions I have stated. [*Ibid.,* cited above, p. 183.]

The issues in the 1953 factional struggle were sharply posed, and they finally led to an international split. It is possible that the split could have been avoided. Cannon was certainly of the opinion that we should try to avoid it. But among other handicaps, it was not possible for the top leaders of the SWP to go abroad. That was during the height of the McCarthyite witch-hunt, and the State Department barred known radicals from leaving the country—unless, of course, they were being deported. Consequently we were unable to argue our case at the congress where the international struggle culminated; and Pablo took factional advantage of this situation.

The divisions occurred along political issues and the fight proceeded along those lines. Nonetheless, Jim considered that a deeper problem was involved—the whole question of party building and what can be done in a conscious way to create the necessary leadership team. Jim, in fact, was of the opinion that it was in this area that Lenin made his greatest contribution.

Jim's thinking on this question is best appreciated in his own words, so I am going to take time to give a rather lengthy quotation from a speech he made November 3, 1953, at a National Committee meeting of the SWP. From this quote, you'll get the essence of Jim on internationalism.

> Leadership is the one unsolved problem of the working class of the entire world. The only barrier between the working class of the world and socialism is the unsolved problem of leadership. That is what is meant by "the question of the party." That is what the *Transitional Program* [the founding resolution of the Fourth International] means when it states that the crisis of the labor movement is the crisis of leadership. That means that until the working class solves the problem of creating the revolutionary party, the conscious expression of the historic process, which can lead the masses in struggle, the issue remains undecided. It is the most important of all questions—the question of the party.
>
> And if our break with Pabloism—as we see it now clearly—if it boils down to one point and is concentrated in one point, that is it: the question of the party. That seems clear to us now, as we have seen the development of Pabloism in action. The essence of Pabloist revisionism is the overthrow of that part of Trotskyism which is today its most vital part—the conception of the crisis of mankind as the crisis of the leadership of the labor movement summed up in the question of the party.
>
> Pabloism aims not only to overthrow Trotskyism; it aims to overthrow that part of Trotskyism which Trotsky learned from Lenin. Lenin's greatest contribution to his whole epoch was his idea and his determined

struggle to build a vanguard party capable of leading the workers in revolution. And he did not confine his theory to the time of his own activity. He went all the way back to 1871, and said that the decisive factor in the defeat of the first proletarian revolution, the Paris Commune, was the absence of the party of the revolutionary Marxist vanguard, capable of giving the mass movement a conscious program and a resolute leadership. It was Trotsky's acceptance of this part of Lenin in 1917 that made Trotsky a Leninist.

That is written into the *Transitional Program,* that Leninist concept of the decisive role of the revolutionary party. And that is what the Pabloites are throwing overboard in favor of the conception that the ideas will somehow filter into the treacherous bureaucracy, the Stalinists or reformists, and in some way or another, "In the Day of the Comet," the socialist revolution will be realized and carried through to conclusion without a revolutionary Marxist, that is, a Leninist-Trotskyist, party. That is the essence of Pabloism. Pabloism is the substitution of a cult and a revelation for a party and a program.

The problem of the party has another aspect. The problem of the party is the problem of the leadership of the party. I believe, that just as the problem of the party is the problem the working class has to solve before the struggle against capitalism can be definitively successful—the problem of the party truly is the problem of the leadership of the party.

You cannot build a revolutionary party without the program. We all know that. In time the program will create the party. But herein is precisely the role of conscious leaders—to save time. Time is "of the essence" in this epoch when years count for centuries. It is certainly difficult to build a party without leadership, without cadres. As a matter of fact, it can't be done.

Look over the world, look over all the experiences of the last quarter of a century, in one country after another, where the writings and teachings of Trotsky were available, where the program was known, and what do you see? Where they lacked the leaders to build the party, where they lacked cadres, the party did not amount to much. On the other hand, those parties which threw up leaders capable of working together as a cadre remained firm and solid and consciously prepared their future.

The leading cadre plays the same decisive role in relation to the party that the party plays in relation to the class. . . .

Given the program, the construction of leading cadres is the key to the construction of revolutionary parties; and the former requires an even higher degree of consciousness and a more deliberate design than the latter. Of course, every party in every generation since the *Communist Manifesto* has had a leadership of a sort. But there has been very little consciousness about its selection, and for that reason, among others, the real problem remained unsolved. The experiences of the past in this respect are rich in lessons on the theme of what not to do.

The present generation of the revolutionary vanguard, which has the benefit of Lenin and Trotsky, has the supreme duty now to examine the tragic mistakes of the past in this respect in order to avoid them and to replace haphazard methods by a conscious theory and a deliberate design in the construction of leading cadres.

First, and perhaps worst, of the kind of party leadership which we have seen and known, even in the Fourth International, is the unplanned leadership of talented individual stars, pulling in opposite directions, squandering their energies in personal rivalries, quarreling over trifles, and incapable of organizing a sensible division of labor. That has been the tragic experience of many sections of the Fourth International, in particular of the French section. I don't know how things are in France today, but I do know that the French section of the Fourth International will never become a real party until it learns to discipline its individual star performers and make them work together.

A second kind of leadership is the leadership of a clique. In every leadership clique there is a certain coordination, a certain organization and division of labor, and it sometimes looks good—while it lasts. But a clique is bound together by personal associations—what Trotsky, who hated cliques, called "chumminess"—and has in it, by that very fact, a fatal flaw—that it can be broken up by personal quarrels. That is the inevitable fate of every political clique.

There is no such thing, and can be no such thing as a permanent clique, no matter what good friends and chums may be drawn together in a tight exclusive circle and say to themselves: "Now we have everything in our hands and we are going to run things fine." The great winds and waves of the class struggle keep beating upon this little clique. Issues arise. Personal difficulties and frictions develop. And then come personal quarrels and squabbles, meaningless faction fights and senseless splits, and the clique ends in disaster. The party cannot be led by a clique. Not for very long, anyway.

There is a third method of leadership which I will confess to you frankly I noticed only after I passed my sixtieth birthday. That is the leadership of a cult. I will admit that I lived sixty years in this world before I stumbled over the fact that there are such things as political cults. I began rubbing my eyes when I saw the Johnsonites[7] operating in our party. I saw a cult bound to a single person, a sort of Messiah. And I thought, "I'll be damned. You're never too old to learn something new."

A cult requires unthinking fools for the rank and file. But that is not all. In order for a cult to exist, it is not enough for a leader to have personal followers—every leader has personal influence more or less—but a cult leader has to be a cultist himself. He has to be a megalomaniac who gets revelations outside the realm of reality. A megalomaniacal cult leader is liable to jump in any direction at any time, and all the cultists automatically follow, as sheep follow the bellwether, even into the slaughterhouse.

That is what happened with the Johnsonites. The cult followed Johnson, not simply for his theory of the Soviet Union—other people have that theory; a lot of people in the world have that theory about "state capitalism." The Johnsonites were personal cultist followers of Johnson as a Messiah; and when he finally gave the signal for them to jump out of this party for reasons known only to himself, but allegedly because of some personal grievance he imagined, of which they had no knowledge and which they had just heard about, they all left the party at the same hour, Eastern Standard Time. That is a cult. The Pabloite cult, like any other, is capable of jumping in any direction at any time, whenever the leader gets a revelation. You cannot trust the party of the workers' vanguard to a cult or a cultist leader.

There is a fourth method of leadership which has been very common. I have seen much of it in my time—that is the leadership of a permanent faction. Here is something that we have to be on our guard about, because we have just gone through a very severe faction fight, and in the course of the fight we have become tightly bound together. It is absolutely necessary for the leadership to see clearly what a temporary faction is, what its legitimate purposes are, what its limits are, and the danger of the faction hardening into permanence.

There is no greater abomination in the workers' political movement than a permanent faction. There is nothing that can demoralize the internal life of a party more efficiently than a permanent faction. You may say: that is contradicted by the experience of Lenin. Didn't he organize a faction in 1903, the Bolshevik faction, and didn't that remain a hard and fast faction all the way up to the revolution? Not entirely. The faction of Lenin, which split with the Mensheviks in 1903, and

7. The Johnsonites were followers of C.L.R. James (1901–), whose pseudonym was J.R. Johnson. A West Indian who was active for a time in the Trotskyist movement in Britain and the United States, James held that the USSR was a capitalist state and opposed defending it against imperialism. He split from the SWP in 1940 as part of Shachtman's faction, rejoined in 1947, and split again in 1951 during the Korean War. James is the author of *The Black Jacobins, World Revolution*, and other books.

subsequently had negotiations with them and at various times united with them in a single party, but nevertheless remained a faction, was a faction only in its outward form.

In the essence of the matter, the nucleus of the Bolshevik Party of the October Revolution was the Lenin Bolshevik faction. It was a party. And the proof of the fact that it was a party and not an exclusive faction of Lenin was that within the Bolshevik faction there were different tendencies. There were left-wing and right-wing Bolsheviks. At times some of them openly polemicized with Lenin. The Bolsheviks even had splits and reunifications among themselves. Lenin did not consider the Bolshevik faction something he was going to keep with him all his life as a closed corporation.

In the decisive days of 1917 when he brought out his April theses,[8] he showed that his conception was really that of a party by uniting with Trotsky, which made all the difference in the world. It was a party action. And a few months later, when Zinoviev and Kamenev, the very closest collaborators of Lenin, went wrong on the insurrection, he combined with Trotsky to smash them. Lenin's faction was in reality a party.

We have seen factions which grew out of a separate struggle, crystallized and hardened, and held together after the issues which brought them into being no longer existed. That happened in the old Communist Party.

Its leading cadre, as a whole, was a fusion of people with different backgrounds. There were the New Yorkers, and some others, who came out of the Socialist Party, whose experience had been in the field of parliamentary socialism, election campaigns, and so on—a purely "political" grouping. Ruthenberg, Lovestone, etc., represented this background. There was another tendency in the party represented by the "Westerners"—those who had a syndicalist background, a background of work in the trade union movement, in strikes, in the "direct action" of the class struggle. Foster, Bill Dunne, Swabeck,[9] myself, etc., represented this origin.

We naturally formed different tendencies—each partly right and partly wrong—and from the beginning we were always in skirmishes with each other. Eventually these tendencies hardened into factions. Then later, after several years of experience, we learned from each other and the real differences narrowed down. But the faction formations remained. Time after time, the two factions would agree on what was to be done, agree on every resolution for the convention, and still the factions would continue to exist.

In such circumstances the factions degenerated into gangs struggling for power, and the degeneration of the Communist Party was greatly facilitated by that. The Comintern should have helped us to unify the cadre, but instead it fed the flames of factionalism in order to fish in the troubled waters to create its own Stalinist faction. Those were bitter times. I began to rebel against that sterile kind of struggle and I made several attempts—years before we were thrown out of the party for Trotskyism—I made several attempts to break up the politically senseless faction formations. A number of us broke away from the Foster gang and formed a separate grouping and

8. "The Tasks of the Proletariat in The Present Revolution," (*Collected Works*, Vol. 24, pp. 21–26) known as the "April Theses," was the resolution submitted by Lenin to an April 1917 conference of the Bolshevik Party. Adoption of the theses set the party on a course toward socialist revolution in Russia.

9. Charles Ruthenburg (1882–1927) was a leader of the Socialist Party left wing, and a founder of the American CP. He was general secretary of the party at his death. Jay Lovestone (1898–) was a founder of the American CP in the 1920s. He became the leader of a rightist faction, which for a time—with Stalin's backing—took control of the party. Stalin's leftward shift in 1929 led to the expulsion of Lovestone and his remaining followers. Lovestone maintained an organization until the opening of World War II. During the cold war he was an organizer of the AFL-CIO's proimperialist and anticommunist activities around the world. Bill Dunne was a leader of the American CP. He remained with the Stalinists after Cannon and three of his brothers (Miles, Grant, and Vincent) were expelled for Trotskyism. Dunne was expelled from the CP at the end of World War II. Arne Swabeck (1890–) was a founder of the American Communist Party, the Communist League of America, and the Socialist Workers Party. He was a leader of the SWP until the 1960s when he became a Maoist. He left the SWP in 1967.

united with a group that Weinstone had split off from the Lovestoneites, with the same revolt against this purposeless gang factionalism. We formed a "middle grouping" with the slogan: "Dissolve the factions."

We carried on a fight for a couple of years to dissolve the factions into the party. But by that time both the Lovestoneites and the Fosterites had become so hardened in the gang and clique spirit that it was impossible to do it. That contributed to the degeneration of the Communist Party, because permanent factions become cliques and they exclude everybody else. If a permanent faction happens to get control of the leadership of the party and runs the party as a faction, it is bound to exclude others from any real place in the leadership. By that very fact it drives the others into the organization of counter-cliques and counter-factions, and there is no longer a single cadre in the leadership of the party. We saw that happen in the CP. We have to learn something from that experience.

In our party, basing ourselves on our experiences and our studies, we have had a conception of the leadership not as a number of uncoordinated individual stars; not as a clique; not, in God's name, as a cult; and not as a permanent faction. Our conception of the leadership is that of a leading cadre.

It is a conscious design, patiently worked at for years and years. A leading cadre, in our conception, has the following basic characteristics: It consists of people who are first of all united on the program, not on every single question that arises in daily work, but on the basic program of Trotskyism. That is the beginning.

The second feature is that the leading cadre is an *inclusive* and not an *exclusive* selection. It does not have a fixed membership, but deliberately keeps the door open all the time for the inclusion of new people, for the assimilation and development of others, so that the leading cadre is flexibly broadening in numbers and in influence all the time [emphasis Cannon's].

Our cadre has another feature. It constructs the National Committee as a widely democratic representation of the party. I do not know how the leadership is constructed in other parties, but our party here is not led exclusively by the central political working group in New York. The leadership, we have always emphasized, is not the Secretariat. It is not the Political Committee. It is not the Editorial Board. It is the National Committee plenum. The plenum includes the Secretariat, the Political Committee, and the Editorial Board, *plus* the leading comrades from all the districts of the party [emphasis Cannon's].

These district representatives, as you know, are not handpicked in New York and promoted by special maneuvers. We all know how to do that sort of thing and deliberately refrain from doing it. The central leaders never interfere with the deliberations of the nominating commission at party conventions. The district representatives are freely selected by the delegates from their districts and confirmed by the nominating commission. They really represent their branches or locals, and when they sit in the plenum you have a really democratic representation of the entire party. That is one reason why our plenums have such a commanding authority in the party.

When the plenum meets, we can say that we are the leadership because we really are. It is a small convention every time we have a plenum of the National Committee. That is part of our deliberate program of constructing a representative leadership which is democratically controlled.

A third feature of our conception of the cadre, which we work on consciously and deliberately all the time, is to cultivate among all the leading people the ability to work together; not to be individual stars; not to be wiseacres who make problems of themselves—but people who fit into a machine; work with others; recognize that there is no such thing as an unimportant person, that anybody who stands for the program and is sent into the National Committee by his branch or local has got something to give. The task of the central leaders of the party is to open the door for him, find out what he can do, and help him to train himself to do better in the future.

The ability to work together is an essential feature of our conception of the leading cadre, and the next feature is that of a division of labor. It is not necessary for one or two wise guys to know everything and do everything. It is much better, much firmer, much surer if you have a broad selection of people, each one of whom contributes something to the decisions and specializes in work for which he is qualified, and coordinates his work with others.

I must say, I take great satisfaction in the way the leading cadre of our party has evolved and developed in the period since the open fight with the Pablo-Cochran[10] revisionists began. I think they have given the world movement a model demonstration of a strong group of people, of varied talents and experiences, learning how to coordinate their efforts, divide the labor between them, and work collectively so that the strength of each one becomes the strength of all. We end up with a powerful machine, which combines the merits of all its individual members into a multiplied power.

And you not only combine the merits and get good out of them. You can sometimes also get good and positive results from a combination of faults. That also takes place in a properly organized and coordinated cadre. That thought was expressed to me in a letter from Trotsky. What I am telling you here is not exclusively what I have seen and experienced and thought up in my own head. It is not only our experience, but also a great deal of *personal instruction from Trotsky* [this and following emphases are Hansen's]. He formed the habit of writing to me very often after he found out that I was willing to listen and did not take offense at friendly criticism.

He kept advising me all the time about the problems of leadership. As far back as 1935 and 1936, in the fight with the Musteites and the Oehlerites,[11] he gave us such advice. He always referred to Lenin, how Lenin had put his cadre together. He said, Lenin would take one man who had an impulse for action, smelled opportunities, and had a tendency to run ahead of himself, and balance him off against a man who was a little more cautious—and the compromise between the two produced a balanced decision, which redounded to the benefit of the party.

He told me, for example, in one letter where he was advising me to be very careful and not to make an exclusive slate for the National Committee, and not to eliminate people who have some faults which I especially don't like, such as hesitation, conciliationism, and indecisiveness in general; he said, you know Lenin used to say about Kamenev, that he was a constitutional vacillator; he always tended at the moment of decision to "soften up," to vacillate and conciliate. Kamenev, as a matter of fact, belonged to the faction of Bolshevik conciliators in the period after 1907 to 1917, with a tendency toward conciliation with the Mensheviks, but he remained in the Bolshevik Party.

And Lenin used to say—as Trotsky explained it to me—we need Kamenev and the

10. Bert Cochran (1916–) joined the Communist League of America in 1934 and later played a prominent role in organizing the Socialist Workers Party's activity in the United Auto Workers union. He became deeply pessimistic about the prospects of the U.S. working class during the McCarthyite witch-hunt and led a split from the party in 1953 in support of Pablo's positions. Cochran's grouping formed the Socialist Union, which broke openly with Trotskyism in mid-1954, splitting with the International Secretariat. His group, which published the magazine *American Socialist*, folded up before the 1960s. Cochran is the author of many books and a resident at Columbia University's Institute on Communist Affairs.

11. In December 1934 the Communist League of America fused with the American Workers Party headed by A.J. Muste (1885–1967), a former Protestant minister and pacifist who became involved in labor organizing. Following the fusion, Cannon proposed orienting toward a left wing that was growing in the Socialist Party. His proposals were opposed by a faction led by Hugo Oehler (1903–), which split from the party in 1935 after failing to win a majority. When Cannon proposed entering the Socialist Party to win over its left wing, Muste was head of a faction that opposed this on tactical grounds, but the entry proposal won a majority and the Trotskyists joined the SP in the spring of 1936. (They were expelled by the reformist leaders in the summer of 1937.) Muste left the Trotskyist movement in the summer of 1936, returning to his ministry and to radical pacifism. At the time of his death he was playing a prominent role in the anti–Vietnam War movement.

Central Committee because his tendency to waver and conciliate is the reflection of a certain tendency of that kind in the party ranks that we want to keep our finger on. When Kamenev speaks we know that there is a certain sentiment within the party of the same kind that we have to take into consideration. And while we do not accept Kamenev's wavering and conciliationism, we go slow and take it into account, because when we move we want to take the whole party with us. If he raises too many objections, we stop awhile and devote a little more time to education in the party ranks to make sure that our ranks will be solid.

Our strength is in our *combination,* both of our faults and of our virtues. That, taken on the whole, is what I call the *cadre concept of leadership.* This cadre, for the last year almost, has been constituted as a faction—that is, the great majority of the cadre. We have engaged in a faction struggle. But what was that cadre organized into a faction for? It was not the whole cadre; it was the majority, but not all. It didn't include the comrades from Buffalo and Youngstown—there were some differences there at first but they have been virtually eliminated in the course of the struggle; the decisions of this plenum are all unanimous. But at the start, the majority of the cadre constituted itself into a faction, meeting by itself, making its own decisions, and so on.

However, this faction was not formed for the purpose of having a faction. It was not formed as a permanent combination of good fellows who are going to stick together from now to doomsday and not let anybody else join. It is not a gang, nor a clan, nor a clique. It is just simply a *politico-military organization* formed for a certain purpose. But what was the purpose? The purpose was to defeat and isolate the revisionist faction of Pablo-Cochran. That aim has been achieved.

That being the case, what is the duty of this faction now? Are we going to hold together for old time's sake, form a sort of "Grand Army of the Republic"—the only ones allowed to wear ribbons, demand special privileges and honors? No. The duty of this faction now is to say: "The task is finished, the faction is no longer needed, and the faction must be dissolved into the party." The leadership of the party belongs henceforth to the cadre as a whole, assembled at this plenum. All problems, all questions for discussion, should be taken directly into the party branches.

I would like to start off this new stage of party life by announcing here in the name of the majority faction of the National Committee its unanimous decision: the majority faction that was formed for the purposes of the struggle, having accomplished its task, hereby dissolves itself into the party. [*Speeches to the Party,* cited above, pp. 202–13.]

I want to emphasize the fact that I left out some sentences and even paragraphs from Jim's comments. If you would like to see what I left out, I would suggest that you buy a copy of the book.

Reunification of the International

Now let me turn to the reunification of the International Secretariat and the International Committee, which occurred in 1963. Jim's role in this was decisive.

A minority of forces on both sides refused to participate in this reunification. On the side of the International Secretariat, the leading figure who split away was Juan Posadas; on the side of the International Committee, Gerry Healy.[12]

Cannon had begun raising the question of reunification right after the Kremlin crushed the incipient political revolution that flared up in

12. Gerry Healy (1915–) was the central leader of the British section at the time of the factional struggle in 1953. He supported the International Committee. Later he opposed the 1963 reunification, using as a pretext the view that Cuba remained capitalist. Healy's primary goal was to protect his undemocratic and increasingly cultist regime in the British section from international scrutiny and influences. After splitting from the Fourth International in 1963, Healy's British grouping (renamed the Workers Revolutionary Party), along with the rump International Committee he sought to maintain, steadily disintegrated. Juan Posadas (Homero Cristali) was an Argentine leader of the International Secretariat's Latin American Bureau. He split from the Fourth International in 1962 advocating that the Soviet Union launch a nuclear war which would end up in the victory of world socialism.

Hungary in 1956. Cannon did this because of the stand taken by the International Secretariat in opposing the Kremlin's action there and in Poland. The stand taken by the International Secretariat was the same as that of the International Committee. The two factions thus had an identical political position on an issue of key importance to the world revolution.

Taking this development in connection with other positions adopted by the International Secretariat, Cannon came to the conclusion that Pablo had retreated, at least temporarily, on the political issues that had led to the factional struggle and that this opened the way for a resolution of the split on the basis of a principled program. It should be noted that Cannon took this view before the victory of the Cuban revolution, on which both factions reached common judgments by and large, especially on the political positions.

Cannon's position can easily be understood in light of his views on the evils of permanent factions and of dead-end factionalism. As he put it in one of his lectures in 1942 on the history of American Trotskyism: "Politics is not religion; political disputes do not remain forever undecided. Life decides."

As an instance of this, one can point to the fact that life had decided as to the validity of Pablo's prognosis that World War III was going to break out on or about 1954.

What caused the long delay of about six years from the time Cannon was prepared to move toward reunification on a principled basis until it was consummated in 1963?

That is a story worth a book in and of itself. At bottom the delay was caused by the dead-end factionalism of two leaders: Gerry Healy on the side of the International Committee and Michel Pablo on the side of the International Secretariat. Both of them paid lip service to the idea of reunification while both of them sabotaged it.

Cannon easily saw through Pablo's tactics. In Healy's case he thought for some time that only errors were involved. Eventually Healy himself had to admit that he was playing a double game, and with the accumulation of further facts, Cannon came to understand to perfection the miserable motives guiding Healy's course of action.

The reunification made possible some new gains for the world Trotskyist movement, particularly in connection with the great protest movement that developed against the role of American imperialism in Vietnam in the 1960s and early seventies.

In 1969 new differences developed in the Fourth International that still remain to be resolved.[13] However, all this constitutes another subject. And none of it would alter our conclusions as to the stature of James P. Cannon as an internationalist. In his final years he did not change. He never considered himself to be more than a disciple of Lenin and Trotsky, although he felt that in at least one field he was an expert—how to apply their teachings to the American sector of the world revolution.

Three stages

Let me recapitulate Cannon's development as an internationalist. It can be divided into three stages.

In the first stage, we find a young American who has the good fortune to gain an understanding of what will be achieved once humanity is able to bring scientific planning into economics on a worldwide scale.

This young person decides to dedicate his life to help achieve this goal, and consciously engages in the class struggle to help bring it about. He does not proceed as a "loner" but as a member of the most militant movement on the scene, the Industrial Workers of the World.

Then the effort breaks down because of international events—the First World War and the collapse of the Second International.

In the second stage of Cannon's development, the situation is righted by a new colossal event, the first successful proletarian revolution. Although the revolution occurs in a single country, it has titanic effect internationally.

13. In 1969, the Fourth International became involved in a debate over party-building perspectives and guerrilla warfare in Latin America. It eventually broadened to other issues and two factions were formed: the International Majority Tendency and the Leninist-Trotskyist Faction, of which Hansen was a leading member. The factions were dissolved in 1978. See *The Leninist Strategy of Party Building: The Debate on Guerrilla Warfare in Latin America* by Joseph Hansen (New York: Pathfinder Press, 1979).

Jim now becomes a Bolshevik. He has advanced qualitatively as an internationalist.

His work as a militant in the cause of the world revolution is now much more effective.

To his previous experience in the class struggle, Cannon has consciously combined what was clearly the most important lesson of the Russian revolution—the need for a combat party built on the Leninist model. Cannon sets out to build such a party in the United States.

This effort likewise breaks down. The causes include most notably the degeneration of the first workers state and the rise of Stalinism coupled with a temporary stabilization of capitalism.

In the third stage, the situation is righted by Jim's becoming acquainted with Trotsky's analyses and program of struggle.

The most salient element in this is the increasingly dialectical view that Cannon has of the interrelationship between the building of a party in any country and the building of an international. Two interrelated processes.

Under Trotsky's direct guidance Cannon comes to appreciate in particular the role that consciousness can play in the selection of leadership, which is the most vital aspect of party building. From an expert in the class struggle itself, Cannon has advanced to an expert in finding openings and points of support in the class struggle for a revolutionary party, and finally he has advanced to an expert in constructing the team of leaders required for a revolutionary party.

After reaching this level, Cannon can be considered to be an internationalist of the first rank.

He continued to learn. He continued to play an active role. But this amounted to bringing all his experience and know-how to bear in concrete situations faced by the Socialist Workers Party and the world Trotskyist movement.

What Cannon sought above all, as I have indicated, was a Fourth International that would conduct itself in such a model way as to offer the maximum assistance in the building of strong national sections; that is, sections endowed with a leadership capable of conducting a proletarian revolution to victory.

Along with this he sought a model Socialist Workers Party, among the best in collaborating with Trotskyist parties and groups in other countries, and likewise among the best in applying international revolutionary lessons to the American scene.

The question might be asked, "How well did Cannon succeed in this, particularly on the international level?"

I think the question is somewhat misleading. The Fourth International consists of the sum of the national leaderships. And the primary test they face is their capacity to build combat parties in their own countries. How well they meet the test will be seen in the period now opening up.

As for Jim, he left some speeches and some writings on the subject. He left his example. And—not without importance—he left some cadres able to start on a higher level than was available to him when he first began.

In closing, I would like to let Jim have the last word, offering some advice to revolutionary socialists when he had reached the age of seventy [from *The First Ten Years of American Communism,* Pathfinder (1973), pp. 388–90 (2010 printing)].

> A revolutionary party begins with ideas representing social reality, and cannot live without them. And such ideas, like money, do not grow on trees. They have to be taken where they can be found and valued for their own sake, regardless of their point of origin. A would-be revolutionist who doesn't recognize this had better quit before he starts.
>
> The original ideas of the modern socialist movement in all countries of the world, including Russia, had to be taken from Marx and Engels, who happened to be Germans. The continuation and development of these "German" ideas into revolutionary action and victory was the work of Russians, Lenin and Trotsky in the first place, who were internationalists and avowed disciples of the great originators. Revolutionary parties which sprang up in all countries of the world after the First World War were inspired by the original German ideas, which had become Russian ideas and actions, and lived on them in their early years.
>
> The same is true of the entire historical period since the death of Lenin in 1924. The analysis of the new and complicated problem

of Stalinism, fascism and the Second World War, and the programmatic ideas for a revolutionary opposition, all came again from the Russians, in this case Trotsky and his collaborators in the Soviet Union.

Of course, it might be flattering to one's personal conceit and sense of national pride—if one is bothered by such anachronistic absurdities at this hour of the clock—to organize a brand new "American" party with homegrown American ideas, new or old. But no such ideas—none that were any good, that is—were to be found in the United States when the first attempt to organize a revolutionary party in this country were made in 1919. They were not to be found when a handful of us made a new beginning in 1928. And they have not been found in the intervening 30-odd years.

To be sure, there have been numerous attempts to improvise a purely American party but they all melted away like last year's snow. That's the way it had to be, for there is no American road separate and apart from the international road. America has produced some great technologists, engineers and professional baseball players, and experts in other fields. But, so far, no creative political thinkers for the age of internationalism.

In this age of internationalism, those who have seriously wanted to build a revolutionary party in this country have had no choice but to look elsewhere for programmatic ideas. [Theodore] Draper says that our espousal of the Trotskyist program in 1928 "helped to perpetuate the dependence of all branches and off-shoots of the American communist movement on the Russian revolution and Russian revolutionaries." That's true. But what of it?

The famous bandit, Willie Sutton, was once asked by a reporter why he specialized exclusively on robbing banks. Willie, a thinking man's thief, answered right off the bat: "Because that's where the money is." In the entire historical period since the collapse of the international socialist movement in the First World War up to the present, revolutionary national parties in every country have had to look to the Russian Revolution and its authentic leaders. That's where the ideas are.

APPENDIX

Not long after giving his talk on "James P. Cannon the Internationalist" in August 1975, Joseph Hansen asked me to read it and see if I had any suggestions to make for a possible expansion of the talk into a longer work. The scope of his talk had been restricted by its form—it could not be longer than an hour and a half or two; furthermore, he had not been able to spend as much time in preparing it as he would have liked, given his interest in the subject. The reason he sought suggestions from me was that I had been the first person to examine Cannon's archives after his death in 1974. I told Comrade Hansen that the Cannon archives did contain quite a bit of material related to the theme of his talk, particularly about the 1930s, and I offered to prepare a list of such material that he could use or consult in expanding his work. He accepted this offer, but since he was unable to return to this project I did not make up the list. Now a decision has been made to publish his talk, and I have been asked to supply, as an appendix to the talk, a selection of documents by Cannon that deal with specific incidents and issues that arose in the 1930s and provide us, in his own words, with his understanding of internationalism at that time. There are of course many such documents, articles, and speeches in the nine books by Cannon published in his lifetime, and many more in the posthumous volumes by him published by Pathfinder Press. The present appendix consists mainly of items that have not been published in any books or pamphlets so far; most have never been published anywhere before. They are printed here by permission of the Library of Social History, New York. I am responsible for the introductory and explanatory notes in the appendix.

George Breitman
MAY 1979

A: Four tests in fifteen years (1932)

In 1932, four years after Cannon, Shachtman, and Abern had been expelled from the American Communist Party for "Trotskyism," the leadership of the Communist League of America, section of the International Left Opposition, was in a severe factional crisis. The small CLA was crippled by factional disputes, and for a while a split between the forces led by Cannon and those led by Shachtman and Abern seemed almost inevitable. This danger was overcome in 1933, thanks above all to Trotsky's initiative.

The nature of this factional crisis and the lessons to be drawn from it will have to be discussed elsewhere. Here it must suffice to note that one of the issues in contention concerned the CLA leadership's attitude toward a group in Europe that was challenging the authority of the International Secretariat and why the CLA leadership had taken relatively long to reach its pro-IS position. Cannon had placed part of the blame for the delay on Shachtman, who had been in charge of the CLA's international relations. Shachtman, Abern, and Glotzer denied Cannon's claim, and in their major document ("The Situation in the American Opposition: Prospect and Retrospect," June 4, 1932) accused Cannon of lacking any real interest in international questions, except when they served factional aims.

Cannon's reply, one part of which took up this accusation, is excerpted below. None of Cannon's article has been printed anywhere until now. It is undated, but was written in the second half of 1932. Vividly, candidly, and modestly, it summarizes what Cannon had concluded about internationalism at the age of forty-two when, he pointed out, he was "still a seeker, a learner" in this field.

3) "Cannon's interest in international questions in general, and in internal disputes of the Opposition abroad in particular, has never been a deep and ardent one, except for the last few months when such an 'interest' was required in the pursuit of factional aims, etc." [From the document by Shachtman, Abern, and Glotzer.][14] In other words—to translate journalistic implication into forthright language—Cannon is a provincial faker who makes use, now and then, of international questions for hometown politics and has no real concern for them otherwise. This is no doubt a very profound observation, but in justice to others, it must be said that here, as is so often the case, Shachtman betrays a sad lack of originality. He reveals himself here once again as a popularizer of the ideas of others rather than a creator, as a propagandist rather than a politician.

The author of this perspicacious character-analysis is the unfortunate Gomez.[15] He devised it in 1928 at the time I was first endeavoring to convince the authors of this document that the international questions raised by the Russian Opposition had to determine the whole course of our group in the future. Gomez first advanced it in personal conversation with Shachtman—since Shachtman was his friend, and he wanted to save him from the evil influences of Cannon. But Shachtman at that time was also my friend, and he told me about it, laughing at the foolish arguments of the foolish Gomez.

The years that followed 1928 have not been kind to Gomez. Even his exploit in leading a mob of Stalinists to break up our meeting at the Labor Temple failed to sustain his political career in the party. He died, so to speak, but his one great idea lived its own life and survived him.

In the lynching campaign against us the idea became a battle-cry of the Stalinists, who sought to avoid a discussion of the platform of the Left Opposition by personal attacks on Cannon and his "motives." Weisbord brought the idea of Gomez to the fringes of the Left Opposition. Bleeker[16] whispered it in the ranks after a friendly talk with Foster. Now Shachtman, Abern, and even Glotzer solemnly advance it as a new thought of their own. That is unjust. If I protest against it, it is not for myself but for Gomez, for I believe in fair play, even to a dead enemy. Shachtman, Abern, and Glotzer cannot plead ignorance of the fact. They cannot be held guiltless of intent to do wrong. They are literary people and they know that plagiarism is a literary crime. Therefore I insist: when you use this argument make acknowledgment to Gomez. Give the poor devil his due.

However, if there are comrades in the League who do not know the history of the party and who seriously and honestly want to be enlightened on my attitude toward internationalism, I will not refuse to answer their questions. Records exist on the subject. The question can be studied and verified on the firmest possible basis—on a basis of established facts.

I was not a patriot during the war. I was a sup-

14. Shachtman, Martin Abern (1898–1949), and Albert Glotzer (1908–) were factional associates of Cannon in the American CP and were expelled with him in 1928. They were founders and leaders of the CLA, the WPUS, and the SWP, until they split away in 1940 to create the short-lived Workers Party. Their differences with Cannon first appeared in 1929, which he refers to here as "picayune quarrels." But they became increasingly serious, almost producing a split in the CLA in 1932–33. For the next six years Shachtman collaborated closely with Cannon and separated himself from Abern, who never reconciled himself with Cannon. In 1939 Shachtman got together with Abern again, in a struggle against Trotsky as well as Cannon. (See Cannon's *The Struggle for a Proletarian Party* and Trotsky's *In Defense of Marxism*.)

15. Manuel Gomez was a leader of the American CP, active for a time in the Mexican CP and secretary of the All-American Anti-Imperialist League. A delegate representing the Foster group at the Sixth World Congress, he was elected to the new executive committee of the Comintern in 1928.

16. Albert Weisbord (1900–1977), leader of the Passaic textile strike in 1926, was expelled from the American CP in 1930 and organized a small group called the Communist League of Struggle (1931–37). At first it claimed to be in agreement with the International Left Opposition and conducted unity negotiations with the CLA. But there were too many political differences and unity was never achieved. He supported the U.S. government in World War II. Sylvia Bleeker, a well-known activist in the New York clothing unions, broke with the CP and joined the CLA in 1930. For a short time she was a supporter of Shachtman in the internal dispute, and later became a leader of the SWP.

porter of the Russian Revolution since 1917. I was a foundation member of the Communist Party which came into existence as a result of the split over international questions. I was not the last one of the American Party leaders to come out in support of the Russian Opposition and its international platform, and I think I have been loyal to that platform.

There is a record of fifteen consecutive years, during which the mainspring of my political work has been internationalism. In that record one can distinguish four decisive occasions when allegiance to the principle of internationalism was tested—1917, 1919, 1928, and 1932. On each occasion I took the international question of the hour as my point of departure and subordinated everything else to it. This is precisely what I have meant during the past year in continually insisting that our position on the international questions had to take precedence over all others, and certainly over the picayune quarrels of three years ago.

The International Resolution of the NC today[17] is not less significant to me than our declaration of 1928, just as my support of the Russian Opposition in 1928, after I had finally grasped the essence of the question, was for me as compulsory as was my support of the Communist International [when it was founded] in 1919. Real internationalism is tested by its consistent manifestations at every turn of events and under all sorts of changing conditions, by the indissoluble connections of one action with another, by the *decisive* prominence one gives to internationalism in all of his activity.

By this I do not maintain that I have been free from fault or error on international questions in the past. My reference is to the fact that international questions have always been paramount for me *in so far as I have clearly grasped them.*

On the other hand I am far from denying a tendency toward provincialism which is inseparable from all Americans who came by the same road that I travelled—that is, by the road of direct participation first in the native American labor movement without international orientation or guidance. I had to acquire internationalism. It took a long time. The process was a painful and difficult one, and very probably remains uncompleted. In this field I am still a seeker, a learner. It is very hard for an American to be a thoroughgoing internationalist in the genuine, not superficial, sense of the word. He is not born with this gift. The difficulties of distance, plus language handicaps, determined, and yet determine for me a slowness of orientation and a difficulty in quickly understanding international questions. (Example: The first stages of the struggle in the Russian Party.[18]) Even then I cannot say that I succeed in grasping more than their general and fundamental aspects. That is one reason why I do not venture to write very often on these subjects.

I do not recommend this slowness of orientation to others. But I wish to warn comrades—especially the young comrades—against a far more serious fault. That is, superficiality and glib facility of expression on the complex questions of other countries and of the world at large. I am willing to grant one contention which Shachtman makes in his document—that the NC as a whole, myself included, delayed as much as he did in taking a position on the disputes in Europe. I will go further and admit that in most cases he was ahead of us, for that is the fact. (When he acted for delay it was to delay the action of the NC against the position he had already taken.)

The ease with which he gains impressions, and the extraordinary facility with which he formulates and expresses them, gave him an advantage in this respect. His Paris letter to Trotsky (Bulletin #2),[19] in which he pronounced judgment with a pompous self-assurance on the most acute conflicts in the International Left Opposition, was written before we had even considered the new

17. This refers to a resolution entitled "On the Situation in the International Left Opposition," adopted by the resident members of the CLA National Committee and published in *The Militant* April 23, 1932. Although Shachtman was at first reluctant to do so, he supported it in June at a meeting of the NC in New York, where it was adopted unanimously.

18. The Russian Communist Party and later the Comintern were arenas of a crucial political and ideological struggle between the Soviet bureaucracy and the new Left Opposition led by Trotsky. The struggle began behind the scenes in 1923 and came into the open in 1924 but it was several years later before Cannon understood its meaning, on which he acted in 1928.

19. Shachtman's letter to Trotsky from Paris, dated December 1, 1931, was printed in CLA *Internal Bulletin,* no. 2, July 1932.

developments. There is no doubt that he reacted quickly. But, very probably, just because of that his judgment was superficial and false through and through, and not simply on one episode or another but on the whole process involved in the struggle. It is a fault, I admit, to be slow on the international questions and to write infrequently about them. But it is far worse to be too quick and to write too much on international questions, or any other questions, without really knowing what you are writing about.

To write an article—or a score of them—on international questions is not in itself a difficult task. Any journalist—and I am also a journalist—can do it and make it look very learned too. All that is needed, for an experienced writer, is a general formula, a few facts and figures, a sprinkling of standard Marxist expressions, a few hours labor—and the job is done. The ill-fated Gomez, for example, wrote scores of articles about China, and the ill-fated Bill Dunne did likewise. I wrote none at all—and for the simple reason that I didn't think I knew enough about it, as indeed I didn't. But when it came to a question of choosing between a Marxist and a Menshevik line on the Chinese revolution, on the basis of the documents in the controversy, it was not Gomez and Dunne—who by that time had established a reputation as "experts" on China—who showed the way. Their journalistic horseplay around the question added nothing and took nothing away from the problem of *thinking out* the questions of the Chinese revolution, and their decisive import for the proletariat of the entire world. The test of internationalism is not the number of journalistic contributions to the subject but the *position* one takes when the facts are at hand.

There is a tendency in the League—which I consider one of the worst tendencies—to talk lengthily and loftily about the great faraway problems (China, Russia, Spain, or anything you want) and to stumble all over the simplest and most elementary local problems of the League. If the great questions of international scope are the decisive criterion, to which one's domestic policy has to be related, then it must be understood as a rule that works both ways. The test of one's understanding of the international problems and lessons is his ability to apply it to the concrete problems at home. To those experts on international problems who complain about the fact that I devote the limited spare time at my disposal[20] too much to articles about the simple and prosaic problems of trade unionism, etc., I have to explain that I do this not so much from choice as from necessity. These questions have to be answered by some one promptly, as they arise. And the most complacent pretenders to "theoretical" education show a surprising wariness in answering them, especially if they appear to present new aspects which haven't been answered before and require some independent thought.

4) The seriousness of a leader's attitude toward internationalism is further tested not only by his own information on the decisive international questions of the day, but also, and even more so, by the efforts he makes to put the necessary information at the disposal of his organization as a whole. I wouldn't give a fig for the revolutionary qualities of an organization in America whose international knowledge and understanding is monopolized by a few experts more or less. The thing is to educate the entire membership on these questions, to realize a collective understanding and participation in the international questions by all the members of the League. Thus, and thus only, can *the movement* become truly internationalist.

Shachtman, as the document under consideration shows, and as his whole conduct has shown, has never seen the problem this way. He is not enough of an organization man, he thinks too much in terms of persons, he is too much of an individualist, to see it this way. That is why he could conduct the office of international representative of the League in such a loose manner, as though it were an affair between him and other individuals in France, in Germany, in Spain, and in Turkey. That is why the initiative and the constant pressure for the issuance of the International Bulletin in English never came from him, and why, despite Shachtman's great facility in foreign languages, the League owes the translation of all this material exclusively to the unobtrusive

20. Because of the CLA's severe financial problems, Cannon at this time was not a paid staff member and earned his living on a job outside of the movement.

and anonymous work of Comrade Gordon.[21]

It was from this point of view—the education of the entire League membership on the international disputes—that I spoke at the [CLA national] conference [in September 1931] on the necessity of translating and sending out in bulletin form all the material, from both sides, on the highly significant disputes with the Italian Bordigists.[22] How otherwise can the League members really know about them and learn from them? Is it sufficient for Shachtman—and possibly also Cannon—to understand this matter?

But my remarks at the conference on the laxity of the NC in translating and sending out the polemics with the Bordigists—for which I held and still hold myself partly responsible as a member of the NC—were taken by Shachtman in a characteristic, that is, in a purely personal way. It is really amazing to read his explanation of the incident. Cannon's remarks were made, he says, "in order to leave the impression that Shachtman was 'concealing' some material on the Italian situation from the membership." How pitiful! How shallow and absurd! And, at the same time, how revealing! Would the proposition lose an iota of its validity if there were no Shachtman and no Cannon, and no sinister "campaign" of the latter against the former?

It is not true, either, that I "promptly forgot" about this matter of educating the League on the disputes with the Bordigists "right after the conference." I haven't forgotten about it yet. And I am not going to forget it, for I hold it vitally necessary for our membership to know for themselves these concrete manifestations of ultraleft sectarianism and the Marxist answer to them, in order that they may be armed for the future and not have to learn in painful experiences of their own what has been realized for them in advance in the experiences of others. It is only due to the fact that Comrade Gordon, upon whom we had to rely for this work of translation, has had his hands more than full that the matter has been so long delayed. I hope it will not be delayed much longer, and my feeling in the matter has nothing whatever to do with the personality of Shachtman one way or another. I am not aware of any differences between us on the disputes with the Bordigists.

5) Our basic differences in approach to serious questions are again illuminated in that paragraph of his document where he takes me to task for failing to express myself on the French trade union dispute in my introduction to *Communism and Syndicalism*.[23] Did he expect that of me then? I do not think so, or, at any rate, if he did he kept it a secret from me. I understood my task to be an *American interpretation* of the pamphlet, especially in relation to the IWW, and so constructed my introduction. That was a year and a half ago, and nobody found fault with the introduction then or afterward. I learn of Shachtman's criticism now for the first time.

But that is a small matter which can be charged off under the heading of polemical "method." If an expression on the French trade union disputes and the persons involved had been in order in that introduction, on what grounds does Shachtman demand that I should have made it? On the sole ground that Shachtman "furnished Comrade Cannon with detailed information about the then situation in the French trade unions, the various tendencies and groups, and particularly the internal situation in the League which had evoked the criticism of Comrade Trotsky." He did this, he says, "for the specific purpose of having it included in the introduction."

Permit me to say in all candor that such information is not sufficient for me to form a conclusive

21. Sam Gordon (1910–) joined the CLA shortly after its formation in 1929 and became a national committee member when it merged with the Musteites to form the Workers Party in 1934. He served as administrative secretary of the Fourth International when its center was moved to the U.S. after the start of World War II. He has lived in England since 1952.

22. The Left Faction of the Italian Communist Party, known as the Bordigists after Amadeo Bordiga (1889–1970), was an exile group that adhered to the Left Opposition in the late 1920s, but found itself increasingly estranged politically in the 1930s. Its ultraleftist rejection of the struggle for democratic demands led to polemics with Trotsky and other ILO leaders, especially after the start of the Spanish revolution in 1931, and to its separation from the ILO in 1932.

23. *Communism and Syndicalism* was the title of a collection of articles by Trotsky published as a pamphlet by the Militant Press in 1931; it is reprinted as part of *Leon Trotsky on the Trade Unions*. Cannon wrote an introduction for the 1931 pamphlet, which was also printed at the time in the *Militant*, February 15, 1931, under the title "American Syndicalism and Problems of Communism." It will be reprinted in a volume of the posthumous Cannon series being published by Pathfinder Press.

judgment on a trade union question in another country, and still less to put the judgment in writing. I did not know that he expected me to do so. He did not inform me of it. But I wouldn't have done it anyway.

In the first place I know very little about the French trade union movement, and the sketchy information of Shachtman—which is all too often sufficient for him—is not sufficient for me. Trotsky's article appeared to me to enunciate principles on the question of party and trade union that are *universally applicable*. But he directed his polemic against unnamed persons. Why should I, without a single document other than Trotsky's article at my disposal, undertake to supplement him?

I couldn't conscientiously do it then. And, furthermore, I cannot do it now, for the simple reason that I do not know to this day how the various groups and individuals in the French [Communist] League formulated their positions in the dispute. For that I need their documents, resolutions, motions, etc., which, up to the present, I have not seen. I am inclined to think that Shachtman's criticism of me for failing to express myself a year and a half ago on the French trade union dispute is an afterthought. But if he wishes to insist upon it he can improve the criticism and bring it up to date: I haven't expressed myself yet.

And in the same paragraph there is another accusation that also strikes me as an afterthought. "We have no doubt," he says, "that precisely in this matter did Cannon allow political considerations to be outweighed by 'personal consideration' of the case of Rosmer[24]—whose fate in the French League Cannon continued to bemoan to Shachtman for months afterward." That part of the quotation which contains a truth in reality understates the matter. I not only bemoaned the fate of Rosmer for "months afterward," but I still bemoan it. I do not by any means put Rosmer in the same category with the careerist chaff of the type of Landau and Naville.[25] Rosmer had a great past. He represented a gigantic moral capital for the French League and the entire International Left Opposition. His loss is not to be taken lightly. I am firmly against him now because I think he failed badly in the test put upon him and has become a center of obstruction to our movement. I came to this position with great reluctance and only after I was thoroughly convinced by his own actions that any form of support to him, direct or indirect, would be damaging to the Left Opposition.

But what does Shachtman mean by "personal consideration"? I saw Rosmer on only one occasion that I remember—at the Fourth Congress of the Comintern [in 1922]. I never spoke to him in my life, and in the personal sense of the word I do not know the man. He was not my "chum." I was under no obligation to "protect" him. I formed my impressions of Rosmer by the positive role he played in the movement in the past. I changed my impressions on the basis of the negative role he is playing now. Where are the "personal considerations"?

To make a distinction between an "old revolutionist" and a parvenu who just arrived from nowhere is not a "personal consideration." It is a sense of discrimination which characterizes every serious revolutionist. If Shachtman could understand this it would aid him in correcting some of the crudest mistakes he made in Europe, and is repeating in the [American] League, in his estimations of the people concerned

24. Alfred Rosmer (1877–1964) had been a top leader of the French CP and a leading member of the Comintern before he was expelled from both in 1924 for opposing their Stalinization. When he joined the French Left Opposition in 1929 and became a member of the ILO's International Bureau in 1930, he was undoubtedly the best-known non-Russian member of the ILO anywhere in the world. He quit the Left Opposition at the end of 1930, because of political and organizational differences with Trotsky, and never rejoined. But he later renewed his personal friendship with Trotsky and collaborated with the movement in France and internationally until after Trotsky's death.

25. Kurt Landau (1903–1937) was an Austrian CP member who joined the Left Opposition in 1928. Later he moved to Germany, where he became the principal leader of the German section when it was reorganized in 1930 and was its representative in the International Bureau in 1930. In 1931 he led a split of his followers from the German section, and thereafter he fought bitterly against the ILO, down to the time when he was murdered by the Stalinists during the Spanish civil war. Pierre Naville (1904–) was an ex-CP member who joined the Left Opposition when it was organized in France and served as a member of the IS throughout most of the thirties. He broke with the Fourth International at the start of World War II and has belonged to a series of centrist groups since then. In 1932 Trotsky (and Cannon) believed that Landau and Naville were trying to make an international bloc with Rosmer to fight against the ILO and the IS.

B: An IS assignment in Europe (1934)

In 1933, the ILO and its sections got a new lease on life when they stopped trying to reform the Communist International and its affiliates and started working to build a new International and new revolutionary parties in all countries. Around the same time the internal crisis of the CLA was resolved, and it began to make progress in all areas. In 1934, it decided, in line with the orientation adopted internationally in 1933, to propose a fusion of the CLA with the left-centrist American Workers Party, led by A.J. Muste. It also made its first significant breakthrough in the labor movement by providing leadership to the militant teamster strikes in Minneapolis. Cannon was prominently involved in both the strikes and the AWP negotiations but he also found time in 1934 for an assignment in Europe as a representative of the International Communist League (the new name of the ILO after it began working for a new International). Cannon had been delegated to Moscow as a representative of the American CP on five different occasions in the 1920s, and, next to Trotsky, was undoubtedly the ICL member with the longest experience in Comintern work. Before 1934 the CLA's representatives to the ILO, its conferences and plenums, had been Shachtman and Swabeck; this was Cannon's first international assignment outside of the U.S. since he had joined the Left Opposition.

The occasion was a meeting of the enlarged plenum of the ICL (its highest body between international conferences) in October 1934. This meeting, held in Paris, was very important because the ICL at that point was faced with a bitter dispute and the possibility of an international split. The dispute concerned the "French turn," which was supported by a majority of the French section and Trotsky and was opposed by a sizeable French minority and several members of the plenum. By October the French section had voted to enter the Socialist Party (SFIO) and had already entered it as a revolutionary faction, but it was not at all certain that this action would be approved by the international organization. As it turned out, two bitter opponents of the French turn did not show up at the plenum to vote against it (Bauer, the IS administrative secretary, and a representative of the Spanish section). Trotsky succeeded in persuading two other opponents (Sneevliet of the Dutch section and Vereecken of the Belgian) that even though they were going to vote against the turn they should do nothing to obstruct or disrupt the experiment that the French section had already started inside the SFIO. The IS also made extra efforts to get maximum attendance at the plenum from sections that supported the turn. Even so, the vote in favor of the turn in the resolution written by Trotsky for the plenum ("The Present Situation in the Labor Movement and the Tasks of the Bolshevik-Leninists," reprinted in *Documents of the Fourth International* and *Writings of Leon Trotsky Supplement 1934–40)* was only six to three. Two of these six were Americans—Cannon representing the CLA, and Earle Birney (E. Robertson) representing the newly constituted Canadian section, which was previously part of the CLA.

There is no evidence that Cannon played any special role at the plenum, but at its conclusion he was handed a special assignment—to conduct negotiations with the "dissidents" over the turn in order to achieve the maximum unity behind the plenum's approval of the French turn and to reduce the impact of any splits that could not be healed immediately. Cannon could not perform any miracles along this line, but he was a good choice for the attempt. After helping to work out the strategy for negotiations with the Minneapolis trucking companies and the Musteites, he had no problem in dealing with comrades who placed their factional interests and dislikes ahead of the needs of the movement. Appealing to reason and avoiding rhetoric and exaggeration, he must have seemed to the factional diehards as an apostle of patience, moderation, and reconciliation; some of them, who would not speak to each other, met with him five or six times at the end of October. And yet he never departed by one inch from the positions adopted by the plenum.

Unfortunately, there was very little about this assignment in the Cannon archives at the time of his death. Cannon had briefly mentioned the plenum and his subsequent visit to Trotsky in the French Alps in his *History of American Trotskyism*, but did not even mention the IS assignment there. The CLA's National Committee minutes of November 8, 1934, giving a summary of Cannon's report on his return to the United States, noted only that he had been "assigned to work on various commissions taking up the question of defining the position of the plenum to the dissident groups and attempting reconciliation where possible." And there was a short letter to Cannon from Trotsky (November 3, 1934), saying that he impatiently awaited word from Cannon about "the important mission the IS gave you. I strongly hope that you have succeeded in settling the matter. The results would justify your trip to Europe two or three times over" *(Writings of Leon Trotsky Supplement 1934–40* [1979], p. 141 [2011 printing]).

Alerted by these references, the Library of Social History kept looking for material on this episode. Finally it found a copy of *Bulletin interieur*, Groupe Bolchevique-Leniniste dans la SFIO, no. 3, November 1934, which contained a French translation of Cannon's report to the IS just before he left Europe. No English original has been located to date, and therefore the report has been retranslated from the French by David Keil for its use here. It is a good example of Cannon's style as a representative of the international movement in the 1930s—calm, methodical, down to earth, concrete, and persuasive.

OCTOBER 31, 1934

Dear Comrades,

As a member of the commission assigned to apply the decision of the plenum in regard to the dissident groups, I had many meetings with the various comrades concerned. Therefore I am submitting a report to you on the discussions and their results.

1. *The Central Committee of the French section.*[26] The Central Committee accepted the resolution of the plenum despite the fact that it contains a criticism of the majority on the international struggle that preceded the plenum. The CC and its leading members, Molinier and Frank, agreed, on the commission's request, to coopt Naville to the CC if he and his group accepted the plenum resolution. In a general way, the CC cooperated with us and facilitated the execution of the IS policy on this question, that is: conciliation and unification with the dissident groups on the basis of the plenum resolution.

2. *The Naville group.*[27] This group having already entered the SFIO, it appears that the differences between it and the majority are limited and that unification with the majority can take place. As stated above, the majority accepted the position of the IS and stated that it was ready to accept the Naville group and give it representation in its leadership.

Preliminary discussions with Comrades Naville and Blasco[28] established that the differences with the majority were not of a principled political character. The real obstacles to unification concern the question of the internal regime and memories of old conflicts which may have arisen in the isolated propaganda-circle existence of the [French Communist] League.

Comrade Naville maintained that the internal regime of the French section is bad and that his

26. This paragraph attests to Cannon's diplomatic gifts. The Central Committee of the French section and its leading members, Raymond Molinier (1904–) and Pierre Frank (1905–), were not at all interested in getting Naville and his group to return to the section after they had walked out following the national conference in August; in fact, Molinier had thrown a fit at the ICL plenum, threatening to resign if the plenum resolution did not eliminate a passage calling for reunification of the section, and on October 29, 1934, two days before Cannon's report to the IS, Molinier wrote a bitter letter to Trotsky accusing him of having "imposed" his position on the Naville group at the plenum and of covering up "the secret diplomacy carried out here by your representative Cannon in order to bring Naville back to our League, *despite himself. . . .*" *(La Crise des Bolcheviks-Leninistes*, published by Molinier in 1939). So when Cannon's report credited the Central Committee with cooperating ("in a general way") it tactfully omitted mentioning how the Molinier group had to be almost bludgeoned into giving verbal assent to a reunification policy that contradicted everything it stood for.

27. The Naville group was opposed to the French turn on tactical and not on principled grounds. But when the national conference in August rejected Naville's position, his group separated itself from the majority as it prepared to enter the SFIO and began functioning as an independent group claiming to represent the old French section. The Molinierist Central Committee tried to deepen and harden the split but was blocked when the ICL plenum in October called for the reunification of the two groups in a common faction inside the SFIO. By the time of Cannon's assignment at the end of October, the members of the Naville group had also entered the SFIO. There they insisted on remaining separate from the majority of the section, who were now called the Bolshevik-Leninist Group. Cannon's efforts failed to bring about a merger of the two groups but may have contributed to the Naville group's decision to collaborate with the Bolshevik-Leninist Group to some extent while orienting toward reunification later. The two groups were not formally united until September 1935, when the SFIO bureaucracy had already begun action to expel the members of both the groups.

28. Blasco was the pseudonym of Pietro Tresso (1893–1944?), a founder of the Italian section in 1930, who spent most of the rest of his life as an activist in the French section. A member of the IS in the 1930s, he was part of the Naville group in 1934–35, and voted against the French turn at the October 1934 plenum. He was a delegate to the founding conference of the Fourth International, where he was elected to its first International Executive Committee. He was murdered during the war, probably by Stalinists.

group's return to the League now would only result in new expulsions and another split. He believed that a certain period should elapse and that new forces should be recruited before the unification. He proposed to maintain a separate group, for the present period, with the aim, however, of establishing friendly collaboration with the French section and establishing the organization's unity later. In no less than six meetings with Comrade Naville, I tried my best to convince him of the danger that maintaining a separate group would lead to new conflicts which could compromise our work in the SFIO, just getting under way, and tend to perpetuate the split rather than heal it. I maintained that new and favorable conditions for unification of the French League, and certain guarantees for normalization of its internal life, already existed. These were: (1) the new field of mass activity opened by the entry into the SFIO; (2) a continuing increase in the influence of our youth [among the Socialist youth]; (3) the intervention of the international organization. I tried to convince Comrade N. that it was decidedly an error to reject unification in these new conditions *in advance;* that a conscientious effort should be made in all these cases and that the international organization should be given another opportunity to examine and supervise the collaboration of the French comrades in a common organization as the plenum resolution recommended.

These efforts were unsuccessful. Finally, the commission addressed a formal letter to Naville asking him and his group to accept the plenum resolution in a disciplined way and stating that special measures would be recommended by the IS to assure a normal regime after unification.

This proposal too was rejected by the N. group. Their resolution will be sent to the IS. As far as I was able to understand, it stipulates that they are in favor of maintaining a separate group, but it states that they agree to collaborate with the official French section under the IS's supervision, and that the aim is unification within a short period of time.

That is where things stand now. The members of the plenum and the national sections can form an opinion on the situation and prospects. In my opinion, the IS, while holding exactly to the plenum resolution and giving its full support to the French section in all its work on this basis, should seize on even the limited possibilities offered by the resolution of the Naville group in order to secure its collaboration with the majority and ease conflicts between them.

The French section now needs a period of freedom from the brand of factionalism and survivals from the past. It needs free rein to concentrate all energies on the concrete tasks inside the SFIO. *It needs a chance to recruit a substantial number of workers from the SFIO.* That will be the fundamental solution to the problem. The plenum resolution furnished the political bases for this development. The international organization should give all possible aid for its early realization.

3. *The Bauer-Lhuillier group.*[29] I also had five or six meetings with Comrades Bauer and Lhuillier. Politically, reconciliation with these comrades is impossible at present, considering their statement that the plenum resolution is false from a principled standpoint and unacceptable.

This group seems disoriented by the international turn of events and contradictory in its positions. This is shown, for example, by Bauer's tendency to go to the SAP with his group (a split-off) and his reproach that we should have joined the London-Amsterdam Bureau.[30] From a political

29. Eugene Bauer (1906–) and Rene Lhuillier (1909–1968) were not really members of a common group, despite Cannon's formulation. Bauer was the leader of the German section in exile and a member of the IS, 1932–34. Lhuillier was a young member of the French section, active in a barbers union. What they shared was the conviction that the French turn was a betrayal of Marxism, which had to be opposed on grounds of principle—which to them was another way of saying they would split rather than accept the turn. Bauer's "leftism" on this point was contradicted by the new virtues he saw in the London-Amsterdam Bureau, the ICL's centrist opponent; but after splitting away a part of the German section and making actual overtures to the centrists, he dropped out of politics. Lhuillier took his small group into the SFIO in the wake of the majority and Navillist entries, but he did not cooperate there with either of these groups and remained inside the SFIO after they were expelled.

30. The SAP (Socialist Workers Party) was a German centrist group created through a split in the German Social Democracy in 1931. After Hitler came to power in 1933, the SAP was taken over by a group of ex-Brandlerites (Right Oppositionists) and for a short time it moved in the direction of collaboration with the Left Opposition in working for a Fourth International. By 1934, however, it had swung back to the right and become a fanatical opponent of a

standpoint, these positions appear to be in direct contradiction with his opposition to entry in the SFIO for principled reasons.

I proposed to Bauer that he not yet take steps further away from us but that he wait until the international outlook becomes clear and perhaps come to the next IS plenum after the French experience in the SFIO can be concretely assessed. His group adopted a resolution in which it offered to stay within the international organization, but our "conditions" were obviously unacceptable.

Following that, I had a final conversation with Bauer, whom I once again pressed to reflect further on these questions and to wait for further developments before closing the door on possible reconciliation with our international organization.

The same with Lhuillier. He promised, while maintaining his separate group, to keep friendly relations with our French section and to abstain from any attacks which might tend to compromise it as a fraction of the SFIO.

In general, a certain lapse of time and experience with work in the SFIO are necessary before reconciliation with these groups will become possible. Already several facts confirm the political line of the majority for entry in the SFIO and refute the arguments of the dissidents. Undoubtedly the coming months will bring stronger proof. That will turn some, if not all, of the dissidents back toward us. It is necessary to keep the door open to them, especially those who have not compromised themselves by hostile acts against us or by going into the camp of centrist opponents.

Fraternally,
J.P. Cannon

new International. The London-Amsterdam Bureau was a grouping of various centrist parties in the 1930s that did not belong to the Second or Third Internationals. Its name was changed several times during the decade, and most of the groups adhering did not last long; the best-known affiliates were the SAP of Germany, the Independent Labour Party of Britain, the Norwegian Labor Party, and the Workers Party of Marxist Unification (POUM) of Spain.

C: The founding of the International (1938)

In the months before the founding of the Fourth International in September 1938, Cannon and the SWP leadership took every possible opportunity to express their conviction that the Fourth International should actually be proclaimed at the coming conference, putting an end to ambiguity about who its adherents and opponents were. Cannon's alertness in spreading this idea whenever he could is illustrated in the following four excerpts from 1938 letters and statements. The third of these excerpts is also notable for showing that Cannon favored subordinating everything else, including short-range or immediate interests of the SWP, to the founding of the Fourth International in 1938.

Following the excerpts are two full letters containing Cannon's impressions of the founding conference, sent to Trotsky after the latter's complaint that he still had not received a report from anyone more than a month after the conference. Cannon did not find it necessary in these letters to discuss the political positions adopted by the conference; he and Trotsky had discussed them at great length in Mexico in March 1938 (see transcripts in *The Transitional Program for Socialist Revolution* and *Writings of Leon Trotsky (1937–38)*), and in correspondence thereafter. In the eyes of both Cannon and Trotsky internationalism could not be reduced to political principles and ideas; it also had to be embodied in people, parties, and an international organization. It was this side of the conference that Cannon's letters concentrated on, so that Trotsky would have a full picture of the work of the conference and the state of the movement.

PROCEEDING TO A ROLL CALL TO THE INTERNATIONAL SECRETARIAT FEBRUARY 9, 1938

Dear Comrades,

At the last meeting of our National Committee, we had information that proposals had been made by the French and Belgian sections to invite the participation of the POUM[31] in the international conference. If this is true, we would like to know what reasons have been given for these proposals.

It was also decided to ask if any proposals had been made for our participation in the conference of the London Bureau. Our organization is opposed to any such idea. We would like to know the status of this question in our international organization. . . .

Fraternally,
J.P. Cannon
National Secretary

FROM DISCUSSIONS IN MEXICO[32] MARCH 20, 1938

Cannon: On the organizational side of the question—shall we consider this conference a provisional gathering or as the actual founding of the Fourth International? The prevailing opinion among us is that we would actually form the Fourth International at this conference. We think that the main elements of the Fourth International are by now crystallized. We should put an end to our negotiations and maneuvers with the centrists and henceforth deal with them as separate and alien groupings.

Trotsky: I agree absolutely with what Comrade Cannon said. I believe you will meet some opposition from Belgium, particularly from Vereecken.[33] For him life consists of discussions; as soon as a decision is arrived at, it is a catastrophe for him. You will also find some element of opposition from the French comrades at the conference. I don't know about the opinion held by the various British comrades, but I agree entirely that it is absolutely naive to postpone. Naturally we are a weak International but we are an International. This International will become strong by our own action, not by maneuvers with other groups. Naturally, we can attract other intermediary groups, but that would be incidental. The general line is our own development. We had a test in Spain for all these intermediary organizations—the POUM was the only important part of the London Bureau and the same POUM proved to be the most disastrous for the Spanish revolution. I believe that our American section should proclaim its position with energy—we have no reason to boast that we are strong, but we are what we are.

Cannon: I think on this point we have to have some explanation for some of the comrades—perhaps in the form of articles or discussions. Some comrades have taken the tactic of maneuvering and making concessions to centrists as a permanent policy, whereas we think that all our maneuvers with the centrists have been exhausted by now. We were justified two, three, or four years ago in delaying organizational actions, in order to complete the maneuvers and experiments with those people, but not now. We noticed in our discussions that there are some comrades who want to carry over the tactic indefinitely—some kinds of maneuvers which are doomed in advance to defeat. And for this reason I believe we have to explain this matter to the comrades. . . .

TO TROTSKY MAY 21, 1938

. . . At the last meeting of the [SWP] Political Committee, it was decided definitely to cancel the

31. The question of the POUM (see note 30) served as a touchstone inside the Movement for the Fourth International (the new name taken by the ICL in 1936) from the start of the Spanish civil war through the founding conference of the Fourth International. The POUM was organized in 1935 through a merger of the Spanish section of the ICL, led by Andres Nin, with the Workers and Peasants Bloc, led by Joaquín Maurín. From its birth it was aligned with the London-Amsterdam Bureau and hostile to the ICL. In January 1936, in its first major act, it endorsed the Spanish People's Front. For this Trotsky condemned its leaders for betraying the working class. When the civil war started later in the year and the POUM experienced an upsurge in influence and membership, several figures prominent in the MFI criticized Trotsky and the IS for their negative attitude to the POUM and urged the MFI to recognize the POUM as the only revolutionary force in Spain despite its mistakes. The divisions in the MFI over this question late in 1936 and in 1937 lined up behind the pro-POUM position all the forces that would soon quit the MFI because they were not in agreement with the founding of the Fourth International. Cannon's letter to the IS was a way of giving notice that the SWP, then only a few weeks old, was going to fight against any pro-POUM tendencies, even if they were presented indirectly.

32. Cannon was part of an SWP delegation that visited Trotsky in Mexico in March 1938. After prolonged discussion of international and American problems, they agreed to work together in preparing the coming international conference.

33. Georges Vereecken (1898–1978) was a leader of the Belgian section and of a sectarian tendency within it. He split from the section in 1935 when it voted to enter the Belgian Labor Party, returned in 1936, and split again in 1938 to express his opposition to the founding of the International.

project of my going to San Francisco,[34] and that the delegation [to the international conference] make immediate preparations to go to Europe. As the decision now stands, I will depart as soon as the necessary funds have been raised. We are now proceeding with this task. . . .

I am extremely sorry about the unprofitable delay in executing the agreed-upon program. Our plenum did not come off as happily as we had calculated. You will see from the minutes of the plenum, which were sent to you, that Comrades Shachtman and Burnham presented separate motions on the action program for the U.S. and also on the labor party question.[35] The real extent of the differences remained obscure to many of the comrades at the plenum, and even to this day we have not arrived at a precise clarification. The subcommittee appointed to draft the action program and the labor party resolution has not yet been able to complete its work. Another session is set for next Monday, at which time I hope we will at least come to a conclusion either to agree or to disagree definitely.[36]

You can understand that this state of affairs could only operate against the prompt departure of the delegation. Even now, many comrades are extremely apprehensive at the prospect of our departure for the congress while the policy of our party for the next period remains indefinite. The party membership know there are some "differences" but do not know what they are. Consequently there is much unrest and dissatisfaction. Many comrades are of the opinion that it would be best to postpone the international congress till this matter is settled here.

Normally I would agree with this opinion. But it seems to me clear, as I remarked in a previous letter, that the too-long smouldering difficulties of the European sections must be brought to a conclusion by congress action, the Fourth International constituted, and the line clearly drawn between adherents and opponents. Besides these general considerations, the American section, having taken the initiative to set preparations [for the international conference] in motion and thereby naturally starting up a final burst of energy from all disintegrating elements, has no right, either political or moral, to leave things hanging in the air. Even "common sense," despite its lack of universality, applies fully here with its excellent maxim: "Don't start anything you can't finish."

Numerous comrades are disturbed about the possible consequences in our party if the delegation is absent while unsettled questions are simmering. You also may feel a certain alarm on this score, but take my word for it—don't worry about the American party. The members will take their time to digest the new proposals, and perhaps some practical work will suffer temporarily during the discussion, but the overwhelming majority will find their way to the right position and decide it firmly.

If our subcommittee meeting Monday discloses the inability for us to agree on a common formulation on the action program and the labor party resolution, I intend to make the following proposals to the PC: 1) That both positions be submitted to the membership in a discussion bulletin, together with an article or two on each side of the question from each of the departing delegates; 2) That the American delegation obligate itself to work unitedly in Europe in the sense of the discussion and agreements with you, and that the differences, or

34. Cannon's projected party-building visit to San Francisco was the subject of a number of Trotsky letters urging him to go to Europe instead (see *Writings of Leon Trotsky (1937–38)*).

35. When they visited Trotsky in March, the SWP leaders agreed to ask their National Committee to sponsor the Transitional Program in the international discussion. But they ran into a hitch at the National Committee plenum at the end of April when almost half of the committee refused to support motions of endorsement made by Cannon and voted in favor of motions by Shachtman and James Burnham (1905–) on the "action program" (Transitional Program) for the U.S. and on the labor party question. The differences over these questions were obscure at the plenum, and remained obscure a month later when Cannon wrote this letter. Were there real political differences involved, or did the Shachtman and Burnham motions only reflect the cautiousness a part of the National Committee felt was warranted when they were confronted with important political changes on which they were being asked to vote quickly? (The Transitional Program demanded a new way of looking at several questions and the labor party proposal involved switching the SWP's position to favor advocacy of such a party.)

36. Shortly after Cannon's letter a subcommittee of the SWP Political Committee met and discovered that there were no serious differences about the Transitional Program and the labor party among the supporters of the Cannon and the Shachtman-Burnham motions at the plenum, and that it would be relatively easy to draft acceptable joint resolutions for the SWP membership discussion.

nuances, on the American application of the general thesis be not made the subject of discussion at the congress. I will be very glad if you will support these proposals; it is still necessary to assure some of our NC members that the burning problems of the European sections, which cry out for immediate solution, will not be complicated by the intrusion of the new developments in the American section. That would spoil everything. We must guarantee at all cost that the full pressure of our party will be exerted unitedly at the congress. I doubt very much whether such disputes as may develop here will require international intervention. In any case they can wait until other, very much more acute problems are disposed of. . . .

TO TROTSKY[37]
JULY 13, 1938

. . . *Belgium*: We have a brief note, without explanation, from Camille,[38] stating that Vereecken resigned from the Belgian party. It is not indicated whether this signifies a split in the organization or simply a personal withdrawal. Perhaps the departure of Vereecken before the [founding] congress is a favorable symptom—the reflection of a general feeling that the world congress will put an end to all political ambiguity and half-and-half organizational relations. This appears to me to be all to the good. The time is fully ripe now for our world organization to draw a clear line between those who are with us and those who are against us. An intimation that we are proceeding now to this roll call may also be useful in resolving the English situation. Certainly, all groups and individuals must understand that after the world congress, which sums up all the experience of the past, there can no longer be more than one section of the Fourth International in any country.

. . . *Holland*: I will wait until my arrival in Paris and consult with the IS before deciding whether to correspond with or visit Sneevliet.[39] After the ultimatistic resolution adopted by the RSAP, there seems to me to be little or no hope of collaboration. Whatever the circumstances, I will be firmly opposed to granting Sneevliet or anyone else an exceptional position within the framework of the Fourth International. Better far a smaller group in any country that is wholly ours than a larger body whose real allegiance is elsewhere. . . .

IMPRESSIONS OF THE FOUNDING CONFERENCE
OCTOBER 12, 1938

Dear Comrade Hansen [Trotsky]:

I give you here a report of my impressions of the conference. Comrades Gould[40] and Shachtman, who took more extensive notes, will provide you with a more comprehensive statistical report and perhaps supplement my impressions with their own.

There were twenty-six delegates from eleven countries. The conference proceeded smoothly and harmoniously and accomplished a great deal of work. The documents of the conference will make a fairly imposing volume.[41] Unanimity was

37. This was written the day before Cannon departed for Europe. After spending around two weeks in England, he then proceeded to Paris early in August.

38. Camille was the pseudonym of Rudolf Klement (1908–1938), administrative secretary of the MFI and in charge of preparations for the founding conference. Around a day or two after Cannon's letter, Klement was kidnapped by the GPU in Paris; his headless body was found in the Seine shortly before the founding conference. This was the "Klement affair" referred to later by Cannon.

39. Henricus Sneevliet (1883–1942) was the leader of the Dutch section of the MFI (RSAP). He walked out of the MFI conference in July 1936 and thereafter consciously steered his party away from the Fourth International. The RSAP's March 1938 resolution declared that it would not participate in the coming international conference unless the IS repudiated the Dutch Bolshevik-Leninist group, whose members had been expelled from the RSAP; agreed to place national decisions ahead of international ones; withdrew slanders against the president of the RSAP (Sneevliet) and made reparations to his honor, etc. (For the RSAP resolution see SWP *Internal Bulletin*, no. 5, August 1938.) Because of the peculiar way the Dutch section had developed, it had been permitted to affiliate to both the London-Amsterdam Bureau and the ICL/MFI, and Sneevliet had participated in the conferences of both; this was the "exceptional position" that Cannon said could no longer be tolerated.

40. Nathan Gould (1913–), national secretary of the Young People's Socialist League (Fourth Internationalist), was an American delegate to the founding conference, along with Cannon and Shachtman. He left the SWP with Shachtman and Burnham in 1940.

41. They are reprinted, along with a version of the minutes, in *Documents of the Fourth International: The Formative Years (1933–40).*

recorded on virtually all of the principal questions. On the two serious points of dispute, the minority was very weak. The minutes will reveal to you the exact figures on the vote. I do not yet have them at hand.

The first of these disputed questions was the objection raised by Craipeau to our position on the Russian question.[42] He remained isolated in his views which are already well known to you. The Polish delegates opposed the formal organization of the Fourth International. However, they received no support. Only two or three small amendments to the program of transitional demands were adopted; they were primarily of a literary character. It is my understanding that copies of the conference documents are to be sent to you.

Method—The work of the conference occupied a full month if we count the work of the commissions which worked from day to day preparing all the questions in advance of the formal sessions of the conference proper.

In view of the unstable political situation and the dangers of the disruption of the conference signalized by the Klement affair, we adopted in the beginning a plan of work to minimize this danger. It was decided to establish commissions whose task would be to digest all questions to come before the conference and try to solve them and prepare appropriate resolutions before the formal opening of the sessions. This method worked very well. It required a great deal of work from day to day. But by proceeding systematically along this line from one question to another, we succeeded in clearing the ground and preparing everything in advance. On questions where general agreement was reached the appropriate documents were prepared for formal ratification by the conference without unnecessary debate or interruption for literary work. On disputed questions the differences were reduced to their essence in the commissions so that they could be clearly posed at the formal conference; consequently the formal conference could proceed without undue loss of time to decisions on one question after another. The danger of unduly prolonging the conference and magnifying the danger of interruption was thus avoided.

Conception—The American delegation proceeded from the start from the point of view that the conference must signify the formal constitution of the Fourth International and result in a clear delineation, politically *and* organizationally, from all other tendencies, elements, groups and individuals. We advanced the conception that the conference must signify a *roll call* of the Fourth International and that all questions and the status of all groups and individuals must be decided there either positively or negatively. An end must be made to all ambiguity whatsoever in the relations of anybody to our international organization. The general acceptance of this conception worked for the best approach to every question and for the general understanding that we are coming now to a showdown—to binding decisions. Of course this was not our invention. Such a general impression was in the air.

The moment it became clear that the conference was to be held in spite of everything, a general tightening of lines was to be seen. Disloyal elements such as Sneevliet and Vereecken understood very well that the time for trifling was at an end, drew the necessary conclusions and remained away from the conference and thereby definitely outside the Fourth International. Others who had been wavering took a definite stand with us. The Commune group of Molinier,[43] which undertook a final maneuver, only succeeded in bringing upon themselves a firmer repulse than ever.

Organization—The statutes which were adopted provide for a representative executive bureau which is invested with full power to speak and act in the name of the international organization. This bureau is to create a secretariat to conduct the administrative work and also provides for a subsecretariat in another country which, in case of a change in the political situation, can replace the secretariat and continue its functions. We encountered a general insistence that an American

42. Yvan Craipeau (1912–) was a leader of the French section's youth work until World War II, and then a principal leader of the section until after the war, when he quit to join various centrist groups. From the mid-thirties he denied that the Soviet Union was a workers' state in any sense or that it should be defended against imperialist attack.

43. *La Commune* was the paper published by the Molinier group after it was expelled in 1935 for violating discipline. An attempted reunification in 1936 led to another split the same year, and the two groups existed and fought each other for another seven years, until they were reunified during World War II. See *The Crisis of the French Section (1935–36).*

comrade must work in Europe during the next period. The conference in fact adopted a motion to this effect.[44] It remains now for the American party to devise ways and means of complying with this demand.

The conference was permeated with the conception that henceforth international discipline must prevail and that no recurrence of the Sneevliet-Vereecken performance can be tolerated. The decisions of the conference and its executive body must be universally carried out.

French section—More time and discussion was spent on this section than on any other. Comrades who attended meetings of the cells reported that the young comrades are very energetic and carry out their activities in a well-organized manner. The leadership gives a contrary impression. It's characterized by a sad amateurishness in all questions of organization. They haven't a single paid functionary. The headquarters remain closed until six o'clock in the evening. They appeared to be far removed from the conception of developing a professional staff and a strong apparatus, without which the political work remains pretty much of a literary exercise.

We were agreeably surprised to find that in spite of all this, we have very many good contacts in the trade unions which could be rapidly improved and expanded if the party would improve its organizational methods and strengthen its staff. The rank and file members are very dissatisfied with the leadership. During our stay in Paris, uninspired resolutions emanating from the ranks corresponded very closely to the critical resolutions adopted by the conference. This resolution, accepted by the leadership after a good deal of resistance from some, makes drastic criticism of the organizational life of the party.

Naville and Rous are now so situated in their personal affairs that they can give virtually full time to party work. Boitel,[45] who is a trade unionist, is apparently the best organizer. He works eight hours a day and this deprives the party of his best energy. We insisted as a minimum that he should devote his full time to the section as organization and trade union director.

On this, as on every other proposal to strengthen the staff and professionalize the leadership, we encountered arguments about the financial poverty of the party. Undoubtedly it will be necessary to organize international aid for the French party—we promised to do our best in this respect—but that will have little meaning unless the French comrades really reorient themselves in the sphere of organization. We had the impression on leaving France, after a month or more of daily pounding on this point, that the French comrades are going to make serious efforts at least to improve their methods of work.

Molinier group—We made a strong effort to reintegrate this group into the POI. Our French leadership put up a strong resistance, but they were overruled and a strong commission of non-French comrades was designated to meet with the Commune group and to probe the possibilities of unification to the bottom. The results of this effort are told in the final resolution adopted by the IS and my supplementary statement which you have already received. (Please let me know if you have received the documents of the conference.)

For my part, I made a determined effort to give the Commune group every possibility to find its way back into our ranks and even to open the door for the eventual rehabilitation of Molinier himself. Comrade Shachtman fully cooperated with me in this endeavor although his attitude from the start was far less optimistic than mine.

A preliminary meeting with a delegation from this group (with Molinier absent) came to nothing because of their failure to categorically define in advance their attitude to the Fourth International and the decisions of its conference. We told them we were not interested in a general discussion of differences. We told them that it was necessary for their organization to define its attitude first. After

44. The conference specifically named Shachtman as the one they wanted to be assigned to Europe. But he still had not gone there by the time World War II began a year later.

45. Jean Rous (1908–) and Joannes Bardin ("Boitel") (1909–) were central leaders of the French section (the POI). Rous was elected to the IEC in 1938 and Bardin was administrative secretary. They led opposing factions after the founding conference, Rous favoring the POI's entry into a new centrist party, Bardin opposing it. Bardin broke with the Fourth International shortly before World War II started, Rous soon after it started.

they would declare solidarity with our principles and a readiness to observe international discipline, we would be prepared to make concrete proposals to facilitate their reintegration. They delayed reply to this demand, and in the meantime the conference was held without their attendance. Finally, before my scheduled departure, Molinier came to see me and brought with him a letter from his organization, which complied more or less with our demands. He insisted that I should remain for another week to participate in the negotiations. I told him that if he meant business, I would. He assured me that he was sincere in his desire to end the conflict and that he was prepared to stand aside from the organization in order to facilitate the fusion.

In the course of several meetings, both formal and informal, I got a picture of this group and especially of its leading personality. This impression was more and more unfavorable.

We offered, in the form of a written resolution of the IS which was handed to them, to accept all their members with the exception of Molinier into the POI. To give them adequate representation on the leading bodies and to give them full rights to participate in the discussion and preparation for the forthcoming conference of the POI. As for Molinier himself, Comrade Shachtman and I proposed that he come to America for at least one year. After that, we stated, if everything went well and he loyally refrained from intervening in the affairs of the united POI, we would personally support a movement for his rehabilitation and readmission. It seems to me that these proposals put him before the acid test.

In a private meeting Comrade Shachtman and I held with him and his brother,[46] we urged him to avail himself of this opportunity to find his way back into our ranks. It availed nothing. He insisted on an official assurance from the IS and even this we construed as a maneuver to discredit his original expulsion and to give him a basis for a renewed struggle against the POI.

Failing to gain this demand from the IS, the delegation of the Commune group at the next formal meeting modified their original agreement to accept the demands of the IS resolution to a declaration to accept it only "as a basis for discussion." Naturally this could only provide the ground for interminable discussion without any preliminary basis of agreement and without any serious perspective of unification. The IS rejected their resolution and terminated the negotiations. It should be borne in mind also that all the negotiations took place under the shadow of the perfidious conduct of the Molinier group in the Klement affair, and their obvious attempt at blackmail in the question of the archives. There is something not healthy, something dirty in the mentality and the methods of Molinier. I am deeply convinced now after my personal experience and personal observations that the definitive negative solution of this case is the best in the long run.

Belgium—About the Belgian section I know only what was reported by Lesoil in the conference. He stated that Vereecken, faced with the showdown at the impending international conference, had resigned from the Belgian party and had taken not more than half a dozen people with him. The organization remains intact. Vereecken will probably gather up a dozen or two individuals who have dropped out of the Belgian section in the past year . . . and continue his interminable literary critical activity. Fortunately this will now be conducted outside our ranks. If he goes with Sneevliet to the London Bureau, all the better. We undertook to impress the Belgian comrades with only one point: that they must now regard the experience with Vereecken as definitely concluded and that they must not entertain any ideas of further discussion, negotiation, etc.

Holland—Sneevliet of course did not appear at the conference, and we made no effort to see him. Comrades Gould and Demby[47] passed through

46. Henri Molinier (1898–1944), Raymond's brother, was one of the leaders of the Commune group. After the two groups were united during the war he was in charge of the section's military activities and was killed during a street battle in Paris.

47. Frank Demby was an American delegate to the international youth conference held in conjunction with the founding conference. He and Gould assisted Cannon as part of an IS delegation in England prior to the founding conference. Before joining the SWP he had been a member of the Field group, then called the League for a Revolutionary Workers Party. B.J. Field was expelled from the New York branch of the CLA for violating discipline in 1932, was readmitted in

Holland a month or so before the conference, and, mistaking them at first for delegates of the Field group, he [Sneevliet] told them about an "international conference" scheduled to be held in Paris between himself, Vereecken, Molinier, and the Fieldites. They quickly informed him that they were not members of the Field group and he said no more on this point. He explained to them that he did not want to have anything to do with our organization because among other things, he did not wish to submit to the dictatorship of Cardenas.[48] We learned later that their "conference" took place in Paris during our stay there.

Victor Serge,[49] who I am told is very busy in those bitter intrigues against us, attended their conference. The latest bulletin of the London Bureau refers to a recent meeting, and lists among those in attendance "groups which have broken away from the Fourth International." If the Molinierists decide to go with Sneevliet and Vereecken to the London Bureau, it will surely be for the best. So far as I could judge, their sole significance to us is the confusion they create by pretending to be a part of the Fourth.

Mexico—The conference ratified the stand taken by the Pan-American conference on the Mexican question.[50] On this, as on all Latin American problems, our work should be greatly reinforced by the arrival soon of Comrade Lebrun.[51] This comrade from Brazil is a member of many years' standing in our movement and prior to that had a considerable experience, including imprisonment as a leading member of the CP in Brazil. He is a very well-informed comrade, a journalist and linguist and at the same time gives a strong impression of seriousness and stability of character.

England—I have written before about the English question. The Edinburgh group, about thirty members, are very conscientious people and very active propagandists. They should be an acquisition to us and should act as a solvent in the united British organization. I think my visit there was fortunate and timely.

Coming from the SLP (the British De Leonist movement)[52] they still retain many sectarian conceptions and habits. They incline more to the James group[53] because of its position on the Labour Party question, and were on the point of making a separate fusion with James. This would have made matters worse than ever as it would have tipped the scales in the sectarian direction.

The Militant group in the past six months had suffered from an unfortunate split led by Lee which resulted in the creation of another group without any principled grounds for the split (the *Workers International News*).[54] This could only introduce confusion and demoralization—the more so since both groups work exclusively in the Labour

1933, and was expelled again in 1934 for violating discipline during a hotel workers' strike.

48. Lazaro Cardenas (1895–1970) was president of Mexico, 1934–40, when he granted Trotsky the right of asylum. Trotsky's factional opponents accused him of being "soft on Cardenas" because he rejected ultraleftist attitudes toward the government advocated by some leaders of the Mexican section.

49. Victor Serge (1890–1947) joined the Left Opposition at its beginning in the Soviet Union in 1923 and was allowed to leave the country in 1936. For a short while he was associated with the MFI, but his sympathy for the POUM and the anarchists in Spain as well as other differences led him to withdraw before the founding conference was held.

50. The Pan-American Committee of the Fourth International was created in the spring of 1938 to help coordinate work in Latin America in preparation for the founding conference. Its stand on the Mexican question is in *Documents of the Fourth International.*

51. A. Lebrun was the pseudonym of Mario Pedrosa (1905–), a leader of the Brazilian section who had long been active in France, was elected to the IEC at the founding conference, and moved to the United States soon after. In the 1940 split, he left the Fourth International with Shachtman.

52. The name of the Edinburgh group was the Revolutionary Socialist Party. Its best known figure was Frank Maitland (1910–). Its members had developed out of the British Socialist Labour Party, which adhered to the conceptions introduced in the U.S. by Daniel De Leon (1852–1914).

53. The official name of the James group was the Revolutionary Socialist League, one of the three groups that united under Cannon's guidance to become the official British section of the Fourth International in 1938. The RSL's secretary was Charles Sumner (1911–1976) but its best-known member was C.L.R. James.

54. The Militant group was a Fourth Internationalist tendency operating inside the British Labour Party; its adherence to the unification agreement in 1938 was signed by Starkey Jackson. The Workers International League, led by Ralph Lee, Jock Haston, Ted Grant, and Gerry Healy, was a small split-off from the Militant group; it refused to participate in the 1938 unification and therefore was unable to attend the founding conference.

Party. At the same time, the Liverpool branch had withdrawn from the Militant group on opportunistic grounds. They wanted to work in the Labour Party simply as a left wing without any international connections.

I spent two days with the Edinburgh comrades and we discussed the question of politics and principles day and night, with only brief intermissions for the inevitable British tea (much stronger than the Russian tea and further ruined by the addition of milk!). I suffered and survived all that for the sake of the revolution. I succeeded in changing their opinions quite radically. This is perhaps more to their credit than to mine, as they are a very scrupulous and honest group of comrades who want to pursue every question to the end, and readily admit an error that is made clear to them. They are real proletarians too.

They agreed that they would experiment with work in the Labour Party by having at least half of their members join, and they would also undertake a more serious and systematic work in the trade unions. Many of them belong to trade unions now, but the hangovers of their fatal DeLeon conception in the trade union question prevented their doing any serious work. They also agreed to refrain from any separate fusion and would only come into a general unification sponsored by the IS.

In the London conference, a week later, I had their support from the start for a general unification. This undoubtedly exerted considerable pressure on the James group.

The political resolution accepted as a basis for unification provided that the *main emphasis* should be placed on work in the Labour Party without making Labour Party membership compulsory upon those comrades who have not been members up till now. This at least provides a definite orientation for the united group. It was the maximum possible. It seemed to me that the most important thing, if we could at least get a correct orientation, was to bring all the comrades together and get them in the habit of functioning in one organization which would be firmly affiliated to the Fourth International. We carried on a strong crusade against irresponsible splits and made it clear that the international conference would do away with the possibility of a multiplicity of groups, and recognize only one section in each country.

I received further support for my work in London from a minority of about seven comrades in the James group, who had been conducting a struggle against the Fieldite tendencies which were manifested by the leadership in both organizational and political questions. Incidentally, the members of this group who had been inclined also to make a fetish of the "independent organization," agreed to join the Labour Party and to give a fair test to the possibilities of fruitful work therein.

The Lee group consists of about thirty, mostly youngsters, who have been deeply poisoned with personal antagonism to the leadership of the Militant group. They attempted to obstruct the unification but were pounded mercilessly at the unification conference, and their ranks were badly shaken. Their attitude was condemned by the international conference.

Shachtman, during his visit in England, also had a session with this group. His opinion is the same as mine—that they will have to submit to the international decision and come into the united British section or suffer a split. It is only necessary for the British section to take a firm and resolute stand in regard to this group, and in no case to acknowledge its legitimacy. Unfortunately, this is easier said than done. The English comrades, alas, are gentlemen. They are not accustomed to our "brutal" (i.e. Bolshevik) treatment of groups who play with splits. However, I think they learned something from our visit, at least they said they did.

I will not attempt to prophesize the outcome of the British experiment in unification. Friction undoubtedly exists, and still worse, there are undoubted differences in conception. Some of the members of the James group were still debating the French turn from the point of view of Field-Oehler. But at any rate, the unification on the one hand, and on the other the manifest strengthening of the authority of the Fourth International following the world congress, provide the most favorable milieu for testing out the people and preparing the way, if necessary, for a selection of forces. (Since the unification the majority of the seceding Liverpool group has joined. So also have some valuable individual comrades who dropped aside during the splits.)

There are a few other points which I want to cover, but I must close now. Perhaps in another letter.

Fraternally,
James P. Cannon

OCTOBER 19, 1938

Dear Comrade Hansen [Trotsky]:

Here are a few additional remarks on the European journey.

PSOP[55]—Before our arrival, the IS had invited the PSOP and the POUM to send "observers" to the conference, and they had accepted.

For our part, we were not much in favor of this kind of "democracy." To invite a sympathetic revolutionary group which is considering affiliation—such as the RSP of Edinburgh—is one thing; to invite political opponents to "observe" our highest and most intimate deliberations, just to show that we are open and aboveboard—that seems to me to be a false democracy. However, the tightening of the lines, prompted by the kidnapping of Klement, obliged the IS to reconsider the invitation and to call all sessions of the conference without visitors. I think the matter was satisfactorily explained to both organizations and left no bad feeling. As an alternative, a commission was appointed to meet with a delegation from the PSOP to give them a report of our proceedings and to discuss questions of collaboration. Both Shachtman and I attended the joint meeting.

We spent several hours in quite friendly discussion. It was very difficult for me, with my general ignorance of French affairs, to get a clear picture of the question of the PSOP. Nobody seems to know even how large it is. The estimates of our own comrades vary from five to fifteen thousand. All are agreed that it is a very heterogeneous organization and the left wing is very susceptible to our influence. In every session of the French commission we urged the adoption of a positive policy toward the PSOP designed to effect a fusion with its left wing. We proposed the sending of a fraction of at least fifty into the PSOP. The leading comrades seemed to show a sad lack of initiative in such fluid situations which require quick decision and action.

They had only a few individual comrades in the PSOP—hardly enough to even be called a small fraction. Nevertheless all reports indicated that this handful of individual comrades were doing effective work. The leadership agreed "in principle" to send in a larger fraction. Every week we raised the question again to inquire how many had been sent in. At the end of five weeks, the decision to enlarge the fraction remained unchanged, but nothing was done to put it into effect.

The French tempo is very slow. However, before we left, I think a half dozen or so comrades had actually been assigned to this work. Unfortunately I did not receive any suggestion from you about the PSOP. If you agree in general with the position we took, I think it would be worthwhile for you to put a little pressure on the French comrades to strengthen the fraction by sending in more people. The French movement needs a success and some new blood to reinvigorate the party and to lift it out of the routine of competition with the Molinierists. It seems to me that the PSOP offers an extremely favorable ground for new blood and fairly quick success.

On the other hand, if nothing is done, there is a danger that pessimistic and liquidationist moods will grow. Craipeau, as you may know, has already proposed not fraction work, but entry into the PSOP. Some of the German comrades and others in the commission expressed the view that if the situation doesn't improve in six months nothing will be left but an entry.

We did our best to combat these sentiments. They seemed to us to express an attitude of discouragement. So far as we could judge the matter, the sending in of a strong fraction while maintaining a completely independent organization and press and involving the PSOP in more and more joint actions, party to party, is the only way to proceed in this case.

Greece—You know about the unification of the two Greek groups. They are about of equal strength, and I feel quite confident in this case that the unification will stick. They were divided only by two questions which can very well be resolved within the framework of one organization by means of an

55. The French Workers and Peasants Socialist Party (PSOP) was created in June 1938 after a centrist group led by Marceau Pivert left the SFIO. It lasted for only little more than a year but its existence precipitated a bitter struggle inside the POI between advocates and opponents of entry in order to win over the PSOP left wing.

international discussion.

One of these questions is concerned with the evaluation of the experience with the Archio-Marxists.[56] The unofficial group maintains that the acceptance of the Archio-Marxists into the international organization of the Bolshevik-Leninists was the "original sin," since this group proved to be non-Bolshevik. They seem to overlook the fact that the experience with the Archio-Marxists eventually resulted in a selection of forces for the Fourth International out of their ranks. The main cadres of both groups and even the majority of their membership were formerly Archio-Marxists, as was admitted in the commission.

The second point of difference concerned the evaluation of the present regime in Greece. The official group characterized it as fascist; the others had a different evaluation.

The resolution of unification which was accepted by the delegates of both groups provides for a unification without resolving these two disputed points. A discussion is provided for in the international bulletin to which all sections will have the right to contribute. I am sure such a discussion will eventually clear up and resolve the disputed questions and have an international educational value also.

The Greek unification may have a beneficial influence in the American movement. Some of the exiled leaders are planning to immigrate to America where we now have some favorable opportunities to develop an organization of Greek workers. Some new intellectual forces capable of journalistic and propaganda work should give a good stimulus to this project.

Scotland—In Glasgow I visited the widow of John MacLean,[57] the famous Scottish revolutionary who was so highly commended by Lenin for his fight against the war. MacLean's daughter and her husband are both members of our organization and the MacLean home is the center of an enthusiastic group of a dozen or so young comrades. Your portrait, painted from a photograph by a local artist—and very well done too—hangs on the wall.

I also had a very nice visit with Emrys Hughes,[58] the editor of the *Glasgow Forward*. He is a fine chap, a very fine chap, too "good" you might say to ever be a Bolshevik. He impressed me as a surviving representative of the best type of prewar British socialists. He believes in fair play and letting every side be heard. It was these sentiments primarily which prompted his protest against the Moscow trials. He is very friendly to you personally and reads all your books. He said he didn't think he could ever be a Bolshevik because he would want the Mensheviks to have their freedom too, and he would not be able to reconcile himself to the kind of suppression that took place in Russia. However, there is no telling what a man like this might do in a crisis which compelled everybody to take sides. With all his "softness," he stood up against the war and served a long prison term without capitulating. When he was released he took up his socialist work where he had left off. I advised the Glasgow comrades, and the leadership among them also, to maintain very friendly relations with him and to utilize his cooperation to the fullest extent possible, especially in the fight against the Stalinists.

Together with James, I visited Fenner Brockway[59] in London. We discussed the Klement affair and the POUM trials mainly. As you probably know, the ILP is turning toward reaffiliation with the Labour Party.

Brockway, the ILP headquarters and everything seemed to exude a faint musty odor of

56. The Archio-Marxists were an independent Greek organization that originated out of a split in the Greek CP in 1924 and that was won over to the ILO in the early 1930s. From 1932 to 1934, they were the Greek section of the ILO, but then they broke away and became part of the London-Amsterdam Bureau. The two Greek groups that united at the founding conference were the United Internationalist Communist Organization and the International Communist League. The new organization was called the Revolutionary Socialist Organization.

57. John MacLean (1879–1923) was a Scottish working-class leader who was imprisoned for his opposition to the First World War. As a leader of the British Socialist Party, he became a member of the Communist International.

58. Emrys Hughes (1894–1969) was editor of the Scottish Labourite paper *Forward*, one of the few journals that printed Trotsky's articles during the Moscow trials. He was later a Labourite member of Parliament.

59. Fenner Brockway (1890–) was a leader of the Independent Labour Party in Britain and an officer of the London-Amsterdam Bureau throughout its existence. The ILP had cancelled its affiliation to the British Labour Party in 1932, and its leaders did not formally return to the Labour Party until after World War II.

yesterday, of the old Sunday school type of righteous and ineffectual socialists.

By accident, I saw Willi Müzenberg[60] twice in Paris cafes. I used to know him quite well, but naturally I avoided a direct encounter. I don't know whether he is completely out of the Stalinist movement or only in eclipse. He looked as prosperous as ever.

Fraternally yours,
James P. Cannon

60. Willi Münzenberg (1889–1940) had been a well known youth organizer and an impresario of the Comintern. He broke with the Comintern in 1938 for reasons that were publicly obscure.

D: Helping the French section (1938–39)

Cannon's concern about the state of the French section was heightened during his stay in Paris before and after the founding conference of the Fourth International, and was sharply expressed in the conference's "Resolution on the Tasks of the French Section," which he helped to write as a member of the commission reviewing the work of the French section (reprinted in *Documents of the Fourth International*). The French section was obviously pivotal for the future of the International as a whole in Europe, and every possible step to revive and strengthen it had to be considered and acted on by the International and its stronger sections. Despite agreement on this at the conference, Cannon saw little or no improvement in the way the French leadership functioned during the Munich crisis and an unsuccessful general strike in the autumn of 1938, after he had returned to the United States; in fact, the principal preoccupation of the French leadership was a factional dispute over the new Workers and Peasants Socialist Party (PSOP), and whether or not to enter it.

Printed below are two letters and a speech showing how Cannon responded to the needs of the French section. The first is a letter from New York to Trotsky, in November 1938, posing the suggestion that Cannon should return to France to help strengthen and reorient the French leadership. When this suggestion met with approval by the IEC, Trotsky, the French leadership and the SWP leadership, the SWP set out to collect from its members a relatively large fund to help the French organization create a full-time staff, stabilize its press, etc. This fund was raised only after an intensive educational campaign inspired the SWP membership to make sacrifices to help their French comrades.

The second selection is a letter to the SWP National Committee written by Cannon a few days after he arrived in Paris in January 1939, just as the French section held a congress that ended in a split over the PSOP entry question. Cannon worked together with the other International Executive Committee members in France, almost all of whom favored entry into the PSOP, as he did, but they were unable to achieve a reunification or even collaboration between the contending factions. Cannon returned to the United States in March after he felt he had completed whatever he could do in France for the time being, but the SWP effort continued, Albert Goldman replacing Cannon in the spring and remaining there until the maelstrom of World War II, starting in September, had decimated both the French section and the faction that had entered the PSOP.

The third selection is a speech Cannon made about his latest mission to France at a membership meeting of the SWP New York Local in April 1939. It is reprinted from the SWP Internal Bulletin, no. 10, June 1939. Although the audiences of the three selections were distinct and different (Trotsky, the SWP leadership, the SWP membership), the thing that unites them is the spirit of internationalism that infused everything Cannon did and said, no matter whom he was addressing.

NOVEMBER 29, 1938

Dear Comrade Hansen [Trotsky],

I am deeply disturbed about the situation of our French section in the turbulent events that are now developing from day to day. We have received from Rous several alarming letters with some documents about their controversy over the PSOP. In the latest letter to Comrade Lebrun, he even speaks about a split. One thing is clear in any case: our section remains divided and hesitant in the face of the great tasks and opportunities, and can move along this line only to catastrophe.

I doubt very much whether even the best advice from afar will suffice to enable our comrades to utilize the situation to the best advantage. Someone from the international organization, who has more experience and authority, must be on the spot to help in the execution of the policy and to press the hesitant comrades of the leadership into action.

We decided at the [November 1939] plenum [of the SWP National Committee], reiterating a previous decision of the Political Committee, that Comrade Trent [Shachtman] would go to France. It has been delayed up till now by financial considerations. In the meantime, the opinion has arisen in the minds of a number of comrades that I should go. I thought over the matter independently the whole weekend, and had more than half come to the same conclusion, before the other comrades expressed themselves in informal conversations in the last two days. Of course, my going would cause certain complications in the party, but in my judgment, not insurmountable ones.

We have just finished a plenum in which it was shown that the leadership is very well consolidated. The spirit in the ranks is pretty good, and all attention is now being concentrated on the campaign for the twice-weekly.[61] In my opinion, this project will be realized in scheduled time, by February 1. Three-fourths of the work of the campaign has already been done. And it is now proceeding more or less automatically to the collection of the fund.

I feel very deeply that we must make every possible effort to prevent a repetition of the Spanish debacle.[62] It will by no means suffice for the Fourth International to explain a French catastrophe by criticizing all other parties and tendencies, without being able to explain what our own particular tendency has done, or tried to do, of a positive nature. If we are not obliged to guarantee a successful revolution, at least we are bound to fight and make a showing which, even in the worst outcome of the fundamental class struggle in France, will unquestionably establish the superiority of the Fourth International in practice as well as in theory.

It seems to me that our section must conquer the PSOP, or a substantial part of it, and prepare the ground to seize upon the coming split in the CP and steer the dissident Stalinist militants on the revolutionary path. That will require, in my opinion, above all, an extremely active and determined policy at every stage of development, and a readiness of the leadership to move quickly and decisively in every new situation.

As I indicated above, and as my feeling has developed even while dictating this letter, I am more than half inclined to accept the commission to go to France if the majority of the [International Executive] Committee so decides. I would like to have your opinion on the matter. I would also like to know if you have written to the French comrades. I would also like to receive from you your general appreciation of the French situation, and at least some kind of an outline of suggested tactics for our section with relation to the PSOP and the movement in general. I personally incline to the following opinion: We must not let the PSOP escape us. If they put too many obstacles in the way of fusion, we should enter the PSOP without ceremony if, as is reported, they are willing to grant us some places on the National Committee and will allow us a reasonable freedom of action.

The worst policy it seems to me—the very worst—is a timid and expectant policy of making empty gestures, and waiting around, without any serious design and will to force developments in a definite direction. As far as I can judge from the letters of Rous, this policy, or more correctly lack of policy, is dominating the majority of the leadership in the French section at the present time. I have very little confidence that it will be changed without some radical pressure from the outside. Moreover, I am dubious of even the strongest pressure, exerted from a distance, being able to affect more than a *formal* change of policy without assuring its execution with energy and will.

Is it not possible, in your opinion, that the great events now breaking can galvanize Rosmer into new activity? It seems to me that his activity, even if limited, with his name in the French movement, would be of inestimable value to our comrades now. Also is it excluded that Pivert,[63] in these surging developments, can be surrounded and pushed or pulled in a direction that will aid the left developments? You know both personalities better than I, but if I were on the ground I would not exclude either possibility, and would devote considerable efforts to realize them.

I await your reply on all these considerations and hope that you will find it possible to answer, if only partially and provisionally, in the next day or two. I am fully conscious that the language difficulties, which would impose strict limitations upon the possibilities of fruitful activity on my part in France, must be considered also in deciding

61. *Socialist Appeal*, the SWP newspaper, was published twice a week from February 1939 until the outbreak of World War II in September.

62. This refers to the Fourth International's inability to build a viable section in Spain after losing its original section when the POUM was formed on the eve of the civil war.

63. Marceau Pivert (1895–1958), who had been an aide of Leon Blum in the first People's Front government, did not move toward the left during the PSOP's short life. In exile, he supported the democratic imperialists in World War II and on returning to France he rejoined the SFIO.

whether it is worthwhile for me to go.

With warmest greetings,

Fraternally,
J.P. Cannon

P.S. Enclosed are copies of the latest letters from Comrade Rous to Comrade Lebrun.

LETTER TO THE SWP NATIONAL COMMITTEE JANUARY 19, 1939

Confidential

Dear Comrades:

I give you here a first preliminary report. First—and most important—things first: Approximately one-half of the members of the POI are entering the PSOP this week. Negotiations regarding the unification of our youth with the youth of the PSOP are pending and will probably be concluded in the near future. Meantime the POI continues its independent existence and publishes its paper and review in full scope.

The congress of the POI took place over the last weekend. I arrived only 36 hours before the congress. The factional situation was very sharp. The congress relationship of forces was: 60 percent for the policy of "organic unification with the PSOP by means of a joint congress"; 40 percent for the policy of *entering* the PSOP. The minority withdrew from the congress after the vote. Both groups announced their readiness to accept the decision of the International Executive Committee. (It should be noted that the IEC on January 8 voted for the policy of entry—the Belgian, German, English, Polish, and the minority of the French voting for; only the majority of the French against.)

Comrade Lesoil[64] of Belgium was here for the congress and appeared there as the representative of the IEC. We worked together hand in hand at every step. The day after the congress we convened a meeting of the IEC. You will receive the resolution. In brief it provides that the minority is permitted to enter the PSOP. The POI, as represented by the majority, may continue to work independently along the lines of the decisions of the congress majority. Each group is given equal status with the other. Both work under the direct supervision and control of the IEC and the IS. The IS coordinates the work of the two groups, promotes conciliation, and prepares the way for eventual reunification on the basis of the experiences of the next immediate period.

I am still studying the situation, but it is already clear to me that the unification with the PSOP must be accomplished in the shortest possible time by the most expedient means, not by a dogmatically preconceived formula. The formula of the majority is not politically realistic under the given circumstances. The relationship of forces speaks against it. We actually have only 300–400 in the POI. The PSOP has 5000–6000. True, ours is a cadre party while the PSOP is a very loose one, newly formed out of the Social Democracy. But the leaders of the PSOP find it quite easy to satisfy their ranks that the demand for a fusion congress is unreasonable. They say: "Let them come into the PSOP and enjoy full democratic rights and participate in the constituent congress next summer or spring." As far as I can learn, the ranks of the PSOP, including those most friendly to us, agree with this position. The campaign of the POI for a unification congress finds no echo among them.

One would think that the majority of the POI leadership would adapt themselves to these sentiments and reformulate their slogans on a more realistic basis. Being politicians, one might say, they would readjust their strategy to serve the main political aim of unification by such means and methods as are possible. But, alas, they are not very good politicians; and many of them are by no means sure they want to get mixed up in a broader organization with the centrist "devils." Bad company leads one to sin.

From what I can judge of the situation in France already—and its main outlines are sufficiently clear—I do not hesitate to say that the *main obstacle* to rapid advances and victories for the Fourth International on a really vast scale is the majority of the leadership of the POI. *In theory* they have rejected sectarianism and can even write you a very good thesis on the question. But in their practices and habits and general mentality they are very bad sectarians. They fear complications and look for all kinds of fancy excuses to avoid them and

64. Leon Lesoil (1892–1942) was a founder of the Belgian section as well as a member of the first IEC. He died in a German concentration camp.

keep standing on one spot with the unsullied banner in their hands. Their sickness might be called "opportunismophobia"—the fear of making an opportunist error. You can imagine their alarm when a hardened and unrepentant sinner like myself drops into their midst. They think it is the Devil's Advocate himself.

It is going to be an interesting fight; in fact it is already going on in full swing and the feathers are flying. They would like a long drawn-out war of theses on an international scale. But I insist that everything has to be resolved *in action in France*, and that in the very near future. The fact that about half of our forces are already joining the PSOP operates powerfully to reinforce my demand for the test of action. It is to be expected that things will happen quickly and that you will soon know the outcome. For my part, I am optimistic of victory, not only as regards the inner difficulties in our own ranks, but also as regards the solution of the problem of the PSOP which depends—one might say exclusively—on the solution of the problem in our own ranks.

I will write you a special report on the PSOP in a short time. I have already had a four-hour discussion with a member of the political bureau of the PSOP and other interviews are being arranged. From comrades and sympathizers in the ranks of the PSOP I have received supplementary information. This much is already clear: The PSOP is *primarily* a workers' organization. It is in a completely fluid state, has many tendencies, a wide internal democracy and, apparently, no firmly crystallized bureaucracy. From this alone—bearing in mind the relationship of forces numerically and the long stagnation of the POI—you can readily draw the conclusion that I am for "entry."

Fraternally,
Martel [Cannon]

THE FRENCH QUESTION APRIL, 1939

Comrades:

The action undertaken by our party on the French question for the past few months is the second serious attempt at international intervention on our part. It is the second time in the ten years we have been battling under the banner of the Fourth International that we have undertaken to give something as well as to receive. The first serious intervention on our part in the international field, that is, in connection with the organization of the world congress, is less than a year old. You all know that we expended great effort, time of leading comrades, and material means in the organization and successful carrying through of the world congress. It is not too much to say that we contributed very heavily to the success of that great historic event. It is not even too much to say that without us it would scarcely have been possible at the time it was victoriously carried through.

Now, I think everybody recognizes that we have been repaid a hundredfold for all the effort and time and sacrifice that we invested in the world congress. That is quite obvious. The formal launching of the Fourth International and the publication of its program throughout the world gave a great impetus to our work in the United States as well as to the movement on an international scale. And it is not surprising now that we should be called upon again, within less than a year, to take the leading part in an attempt to aid that section of our international movement which is in the most acute position. Our French section occupies the crucial place on the front-line battleground of the whole world movement today.

Our party in many respects has been the most favored one in the whole international movement. We have had comparatively good conditions for the uninterrupted development of our work. It so happened, whether by accident or not, that our party carried over from the past the richest inheritance in the shape of experienced cadres. By this we were able to maintain the continuity of the movement and to bring over to the Fourth International the priceless experience of the movement that had preceded it. Then again, an item of no small importance for which we deserve no credit whatever—we live and work in the richest country in the world. Material means at our disposal, thanks to the richness of our country from which we get a few crumbs, enable us to make contributions which are impossible for comrades functioning in countries where the crisis of capitalism bears down more heavily upon the workers.

Now, the development of the whole French situation to the point of the most acute crisis when it became obvious to all political observers that we were approaching the final showdown, put upon our party an extraordinary obligation. It placed before us a real test of our internationalism. And by and large, I think we can say we tried at least to live up to our obligations, and we are still trying to do so.

We made a general estimate of the French situation concerning which there could be little disagreement among us. First, we had to recognize the development of events in France as crucial for the whole of Europe for perhaps years to come—to a certain extent also for us in this country. We recognized that a showdown was near. The social crisis of French capitalism was proven insoluble on the present existing basis. We saw the structure of democratic capitalism crumbling to pieces before the eyes of the whole world. We saw that horrible farce of the People's Front, which had demoralized the masses for so long, going down in the most shameful and most disgraceful catastrophe—decisive events in which the forces of the proletariat and the forces of the fascists would confront each other in the decisive battle, complicated by the imminent danger of war, were impending. Either war or fascism, or what is perhaps more likely, both of them together—the inescapable problem of fascism arising in direct connection with the war—was there before us.

I think we all understood that it was necessary for the Fourth International and all of its sections to rally around our French section and give them all possible assistance to put up a struggle, even though we would be defeated in this struggle—and we can never guarantee victory either in a revolution or in an incidental undertaking on the road to the revolution—even though we should be defeated, we would leave behind us a tradition of struggle in France which would prepare the workers for tomorrow. And even if the workers of France should be decisively defeated in the immediate engagement, we do not see the tomorrow as so far away. We know that capitalism has come to such a point in its crisis, in its death agony, that neither war nor fascism nor both together can do other than further aggravate the crisis and prepare for the coming inevitable explosion which will bring with it the victory of the proletariat. The death agony of capitalism, whatever the incidents along the road, however the course of its development may be deferred temporarily, leads only to the revolution and to the ultimate victory of the proletariat. That is the goal we always have to keep in mind and for which we always have to prepare in moments of defeat as well as in success.

Now, back in November and December, our National Committee began to take a much livelier interest than ever before in the French question. We all recognized its crucial importance. We began to recognize more clearly and more decisively than before our international duty, our obligation to the French section of the Fourth International as that sector of our international movement that was in the line of fire.

We got everything from the Fourth International. The Fourth International supplied us with our principles which are the breath of life of our movement. The Fourth International is the inspiration which keeps the wheels turning in the American party. The Fourth International is the staves which keep the barrel together, and we do not dare to forget it for one moment. And it was not too early for us to begin last November and December, following the world congress, to think seriously of giving something back for all the rich gifts we have received from the Fourth International; to give not only comments and analysis, but to give also in practical deeds and actions; to try by our intervention, by our efforts, and by our sacrifices to influence the course of events, not merely to talk about them and write about them.

It is not so much to our credit that we let the Spanish revolution go by in the capacity of observers and commentators—rich and valuable as these comments were. We would have perhaps done better if we had tried to intervene more actively, aggressively, and directly in the Spanish events. Among ourselves, we don't need to conceal the fact that we were perhaps the one group in this country that made the least effort at direct intervention in Spain. The Lovestoneites for a while had a representative there; the Oehlerites had a couple. Even Weisbord paid a fleeting visit to Spain. The American section of the Fourth International, the strongest and most adequately equipped one, didn't do so.

It was high time that we should try to make a better showing in the way of direct intervention and direct assistance to the French comrades. And that was not merely an altruistic decision of our National Committee. It was not even exclusively an action of solidarity with the international movement. In the strictest sense of the term, it was the best kind of practical politics on the national field. Because if we have a success in France, if we have a struggle, or if only one step forward is made in France by the help of the American movement, we shall be the gainers a hundred times over.

And in connection with this decision of our National Committee, we saw the most magnificent response of our party comrades that we have ever seen. We had a revelation for the first time of how deeply the rank and file of our movement is inspired by the sentiment of internationalism; how far it is prepared to go in the form of sacrifices and efforts, far beyond the normal capacity to afford, when there is a difficult action in a crucial situation. That shows the revolutionary spirit of our party, no matter what any pessimists or babblers say about it. It was best epitomized by the remark of Comrade Dunne[65] in Minneapolis in connection with the extraordinary efforts made by the Minneapolis comrades in the French affair. He said, "That is only a small token payment on the great debt that we owe to the Fourth International."

We will never have any cause to regret those efforts and sacrifices. Impulsive and generous response in a critical situation is always and everywhere the genuine mark of the revolutionist. And even if our efforts in this immediate situation were not as successful in the immediate sense as we hoped—and that unfortunately is the case—nothing has been wasted and nothing has been lost. The rich results will yet come in spite of everything.

I think that we were correct in our impulsive revolutionary response to the French crisis. But it appears to me after some experience at first hand on the ground in France, that our analysis of the situation as of last November and December was not free from error. We tended to see perhaps what we wanted to see in the French general strike [of November 1938]—the beginning of a new wave of revolutionary struggle of the masses, which might be compared to the events of June 1936. At a distance it was hard to know that this was not the case, but it didn't take me long on the ground to see a different picture. The general strike was a far deeper and more disastrous debacle even than we saw it from this country. From all indications in the weeks that followed the strike, it could not be properly analyzed as a beginning of a new advance of the workers. Rather it appeared as a rearguard action that was not only betrayed by the leaders but also never wholeheartedly engaged in by the masses.

The labor movement of France is and has been for some time in a very deep slump. Well-informed trade unionists who follow closely the trend of affairs in the labor movement gave me a number of facts and figures to show that the trade union movement, which had reached a total membership of approximately 5 million following the days of June 1936, had receded back to no more than 2 million at the present time. The masses, discouraged and disillusioned and demoralized by the betrayals and defeats and double-crossings, have been leaving the trade unions in great droves. This began even before the general strike. The great apathy of the workers is the true picture of France today. We don't see any class struggle actions. We see reaction in full swing in the political life in France—the parliamentary regime assuming more and more a role of Bonapartism by decree without even the control of parliament. All those signs and symptoms that were seen in Germany in the period when democratic capitalism was sliding over to fascism are to be seen in France with the single difference that the pace is even more accelerated there. The People's Front has served its purpose to demoralize the workers and leave them helpless before this onslaught of reaction. The workers of France have literally been stifled by their organizations—by the Communist and Socialist Parties and the reformist trade unions.

And then during the period that I was there we could feel the weight of this pessimism and discouragement in the very atmosphere in the country. On the top of that came the final catastrophe of the Spanish defeat and the fall of Bar-

65. Vincent R. Dunne (1890–1970), a leader of the Minneapolis teamsters and member of the SWP National Committee, had been a close collaborator of Cannon's since their early days in the IWW.

celona.[66] More than a half million refugees were coming into France and into Paris, and the whole atmosphere—I must say because we want to know the real situation as it is—the atmosphere was one of defeat and discouragement.

Now it appeared to me that the majority of the leaders of our French section, the POI, tended to misinterpret the situation and its significance. The fact that reaction is on the offensive, which is indubitable, and that the masses at the moment are discouraged led some comrades to take a defeatist view even of the perspectives. They did not see, as we saw and as we understand, that all this sweep of reaction, which is taking away from the masses all that they gained in the strikes of 1936, is only preparing the ground for new colossal explosions. We analyzed the situation in brief, that the decisive battles in France are yet to come. Others—although I did not find anybody to frankly state that, it could be deduced from their politics—tended to take the position that the battle in France is already lost. And naturally, from this conflicting view of the situation, irreconcilably opposing conclusions can only be drawn.

In spite of the general reaction and the general discouragement and apathy of the trade union movement, we have to recognize in France that in the last year there has been one significant development in the camp of the politically organized workers. That is, a split in the Socialist Party in France and the formation of a new organization, the PSOP. This was a split toward the left which was the result of a revolutionary impulse in the ranks against the People's Front and all it signifies.

Now the PSOP, of course, began to take shape as a centrist organization. But from our point of view, that is, from the point of view of the Executive Committee of the Fourth International and from the point of view of our National Committee also, such a phenomenon—the split of a reformist party and the formation of a centrist organization—presents a two-sided picture. It has a duplicate aspect all the time. One can see in it an obstacle to the development of a revolutionary organization. A new organization with an essentially radical program but not a true revolutionary direction can even become an insurmountable obstacle.

But it is not only an obstacle to one who sees things from the point of view of Bolshevism, and that is the only point of view worth anything in politics. It is not only an obstacle but an opportunity, for it represents the breaking loose of some thousands of workers from their reformist moorings under conditions where they become more susceptible to revolutionary influences. And if it is possible for the revolutionary party to understand the situation, and not to permit it to escape from its grasp, it can become the opportunity for a step forward, as was the case twice in the history of our American movement.

On the one hand, the PSOP can become a new POUM on the order of the Spanish party and thereby can destroy the revolutionary prospects as surely as did the POUM in Spain. But if the PSOP, or substantial parts of it, can be fused with the French section of the Fourth International, and if out of it can arise an expanded section of our international movement in France, it can be the means of successfully leading the revolution, or in any case of conducting a struggle that will prepare the victory for tomorrow.

Now, as we saw it, the PSOP was nearest to us of all tendencies in the labor movement, in the sense that they represented a grouping of workers who, for the most part, were trying to find themselves in a revolutionary movement. And that indicated to us what was necessarily the next step of our movement—to make a fusion of our section with the revolutionary elements of the PSOP and with those elements who wanted to be revolutionary.

Here began the first of the difficulties in France. The difficulty, I must say in my firm opinion, was not in the general situation. The difficulty was in ourselves—that the leadership of our French section, unfortunately, very unfortunately, was not ready to carry out an active, aggressive policy in the face of this phenomenon. Our French section is not only weak in numbers, but still worse, its leadership is weak in its understanding of the aggressive nature of Bolshevik politics. That is the root of all the evil in France.

The French party, after its emergence from the Socialist Party of France, was immediately hit by a paralyzing split in its own ranks. It has remained

66. Barcelona fell to the Spanish fascists at the end of January 1939; by March the civil war was finished.

pretty much in isolation and has fallen into a policy of sectarianism of the second degree. That is my own terminology; I use that term to distinguish from sectarianism in principle. The French comrades settled accounts with sectarianism in principle in 1934 and rejected it in principle. Since that time, I don't doubt, they have written some excellent theses and articles about it. But in spite of that, by and large the French organization—at least its leadership—remained sectarian in their mentality, in their tendency to run away from complicated situations, to find a more peaceful uninterrupted routine activity, whereas the nature of Bolshevism is aggressive, always looking for some new perspective or possibility to enlarge its influence and engrave its ideas on a wider circle.

Now, we have to make allowances for that in France as in other sections. The leadership in France is without a broad political experience, which is more or less a reflection of the general weakness of the European movement. The downfall of the Comintern brought with it the most devastating consequences. The whole generation of leaders were corrupted by Stalinism or fell by the wayside. None of them came over or remained with the French section of the Left Opposition. None of the experiences of the old movement were embodied in the personnel of its leading cadres. The POI has always been isolated from the mass movement—even from sections of it; and did not, under those conditions, develop an experienced staff of sufficient self-confidence and flexibility to respond immediately to new opportunities and to plunge into new conflicts.

Now, these weaknesses, and above all the failure to understand the aggressive, political methods of Bolshevism, paralyzed the POI at the moment of its opportunity. There was no chance to lead a revolution in France in the last period, nor even—as far as I could judge—to lead any significant actions of the workers. But there was and is a real opportunity for the French section of the Fourth International to connect itself with a much larger body of workers in ferment and motion, to draw them into the Fourth International and expand the base of our movement in preparation for a new rise of the class struggle that is to come.

And not even the intervention of the Executive Committee of the Fourth International, plus the intervention of our party through a direct representative, was able to solve that problem at one stroke.

The circumstances dictated a fusion of the POI and the PSOP—that is politically absolutely clear. Everybody agreed upon that. Here was a centrist organization breaking from Social Democracy and proclaiming its desire to make a revolution, an organization with about 7,000 members even after it had sloughed off more than half of its membership in the September crisis and the general strike—on the other side—a section of the Fourth International—400–500 members, isolated from the masses.

As I say, everybody agreed on that. The Executive Committee of the Fourth International, Comrade Trotsky, our National Committee and both factions of the POI—the majority and the minority—all agreed on the necessity of the fusion of the POI and PSOP. But they agreed upon it in a different way. At least, so they all said. But many times when I heard the majority of the POI proclaiming its desire for fusion, I thought of the story of the professional loafer who used to look for work and pray to God he wouldn't find it. They were for fusion with the calm assurance that it would never come about.

The political problem existed in how under the given circumstances was it possible to realize the slogan of fusion. And here there wasn't agreement. Fusion by a joint congress of the two organizations—that was the slogan and demand of the majority of the POI. The only trouble with that slogan was that it was not realistic. First of all, the relationship of forces between the two organizations deprived it of realism—about 7,000 members in one organization and not more than 500 in the other. It wasn't realistic for the smaller organization to demand a joint congress.

Secondly, the PSOP had just a few months previously held its founding congress. The leaders of the PSOP had an easy answer to the members of their own rank and file who wanted to come together with our people. They said: "We just had a congress a few months ago. We are going to have another one in May. We haven't yet adopted our program. Let these Trotskyites come in—join our party and have the democratic rights of everybody else." And that seemed a perfectly reasonable and rational answer. The slogan of the POI created no response in the ranks of the PSOP. It reacted, as a matter of fact, against us and not in our favor.

Now fusion of the POI and the PSOP in the given circumstances in France could be and can be realized only by entry of our organization into the larger one. There is no other way. The more formalities and conditions that we put even for entry, the more we build fences around ourselves. That coincides entirely with the wishes of the elements of the leadership who don't want us in. The thing to do, very obviously in my opinion, which was also the opinion of the Executive Committee of the Fourth International, was to enter the centrist organization without ceremony or conditions, and then create in that organization means to conduct our work.

Shortly before I arrived in France, the Executive Committee of the Fourth International held a meeting and adopted such a recommendation—recommending to the POI that it should join the PSOP.

It seemed to me, normally the recommendation of the Fourth International should have sufficed. It is not pleasant to contemplate that the recommendation of our International Executive Committee does not carry a great weight in the affairs of any single section. I am sure our party would hesitate ten times over in rejecting a recommendation that came with such authority. But it seemed to have no bearing in the POI. A faction fight was raging and the ranks were divided into majority and minority factions.

I arrived a day and a half before the congress was called. It was held in an atmosphere of sharp factionalism and antagonism—with a split impending. I must say that I wasn't received with too much enthusiasm by the majority. Before I had a moment to say anything, they expected me to be on the side of the liquidators and opportunists, as they called the entrist faction. At any rate, I didn't try to influence very much the decisions of the congress. That would have been impossible in such a short time anyway. Together with comrade Lesoil of Belgium who had been sent by the [International] Executive Committee as representative to the congress—he and I together tried to use our influence to moderate the faction atmosphere, to eliminate organizational and technical disputes which might sharpen the atmosphere. In general we worked for a policy of moderation.

We had a pretty clear impression of the results of the congress the day before. The factions were pretty well defined and it appeared on the face of things that the opponents of entry would have about 60 percent and the minority 40 percent. The minority claimed that many delegations were not quite correct and they intended to contest a number and to dispute the majority of the congress. We prevailed upon them not to do that, not to press their contest to the point of split in the congress before the political question would be discussed, and in general, as I said, worked to moderate the atmosphere. The result of the congress in spite of that—in spite of the fact that the minority forewent its contest on delegates—showed a relationship of forces of 60 percent against entry and 40 percent in favor of it.

I don't know, and I don't know whether anybody knows, the exact proportions. But in any case I know that was the minimum strength of the minority—40 percent. And without our knowledge, and without our intervention after the votes had been taken, the minority walked out of the congress anyhow and announced its intention to join the PSOP.

We decided to await developments, and since it was manifestly impossible to solve the problem at one stroke, to work towards the solution of the problem in sections—first with the minority favoring entry into the PSOP, and secondly, perhaps, with the youth. In any case, it was clearly going to be a drawn-out process and could not be brought to a conclusion at one stroke.

The intervening period gave me a good opportunity to make a closer study of the PSOP and this is substantially what I found out about it. It was estimated during that period that it was 5,000 or 6,000 strong. It had originally about 20,000 members. In the September war crisis, the general strike, and other events it had lost over half or three-fourths of its membership who had fallen out or gone back to the Socialist Party. We found out later, through the investigations of our comrades who joined the PSOP, that it actually has no less than 7,000 members. In the city of Paris it has 145 branches and has organizations in all the provinces of France.

The general composition of the party is not so

bad. About half, perhaps, are workers. The other half, I don't know what they call them in France—white collar people and professors and so on—an awful lot of professors. And, unfortunately, most of them are not of the revolutionary variety, as with us, but more of the petty-bourgeois type. There is a joke they tell around there—that the PSOP really means the Socialist Party of Workers and Professors. For the most part, these petty-bourgeois pedants exert a conservative influence in the organization and play a role out of all proportion to their rights. This is partly due to the peculiar tradition of the French movement, which does not develop the professional functionary. And that is regarded by the Frenchmen as a wonderful democratic situation. They don't have a lot of bureaucrats taking up the payments of the membership, sitting around and doing nothing except giving orders. The leaders of the party are people who have free time to give—leaders in their spare time. This system is the opposite to that of the Bolshevik party which trains a professional staff and gives it the leadership of the movement. That is the tradition of Bolshevism.

I had argued with some of the PSOP leaders on that question. In that great party of 7,000 members they have, if I remember correctly, one functionary—a technical man and not a political leader. The leaders of the Socialist Party in this country before the war were of the same type. They were primarily generous professors, lawyers, and preachers who had time to spare. The functionary of the party who gave his whole time was simply the drudge who carried out the orders. The real bosses who really ran the party were not giving their whole time to it. We put a stop to this monkey-business when we formed the CP in 1919; it has no part in our tradition. I discussed this question with some of the leaders of the PSOP. Our party, which is smaller than theirs, has approximately thirty full-time functionaries in the party and youth. It seemed incomprehensible to them. And yet one has to wonder how it is possible to conceive of making a revolution without a professional staff.

The party has an enormous amount of agitational energy, has innumerable meetings, publishes a weekly paper of 20,000 circulation, has a movie department—in general it creates the impression of a very active agitational party which is extremely superficial in its theory. Such a party, if it has a cadre of Bolsheviks and is equipped with a theoretical direction, can develop. But if left to develop by itself, it can be smashed at one blow.

The leadership has at least three definite currents, although I don't think they are organized into factions. They have a right wing, close in its ideology to the Socialist Party of France. The great bloc of the center, which is represented more by Pivert, has very much the ideology of the London Bureau. The left wing, which is not too strong, inclines very much towards cooperation with the Trotskyites, is very anxious to have the Trotskyites in the party, but is by no means Bolshevik. On the whole, I would say it is a much better party than the Socialist Party of the United States when we entered—much better in its composition, its activity, its freshness, and its leadership. It is a far more promising field of revolutionary development. The PSOP is, of course, a centrist party in the real sense of the term. But every centrist organization is different. This is a centrist organization which has only recently broken from the Social Democracy and is impelled by the violence of the split on a left-wing course. United with a genuine left wing grouping it can finish its development. Left to itself, it can swing back to its point of departure.

The London Bureau is interested also in its course. And the London Bureau represents a variety of centrism which on the surface may appear to be identical with that of the PSOP but which is far worse—it is, in large part, the centrism of ex-Communists slipping back into the direction of reformism and of old hardened bureaucrats incapable of responding to revolutionary activity. I consider that the PSOP has the prospect of becoming another POUM without difficulty, and of sharing its fate. On the other hand, fertilized by the doctrines of the Fourth International and influenced by its cadres within, a large part of the PSOP can be brought on the path of the Fourth International and can stand at the head of the French masses in the coming revolutionary struggles.

And that, as far as I could judge, and as far as any qualified political representative of the Executive Committee of the Fourth International could judge—that problem is the main and crucial problem of the French section of the Fourth International.

From a political point of view we are not only responsible for the POI. We bear a certain responsibility also for the PSOP. It depends on the Fourth International in no small degree what will be its further development—which direction it will take.

I found it possible without difficulty, in fact, without any solicitation on my part, to have numerous discussions with various leading figures of the PSOP. Of course, at the time I went we had great hopes that our French section would respond to the political necessities of the moment. We hoped they would be ready to act in a way determined by political necessity, and that I would, perhaps, be useful as a result of our experience in such matters, in negotiating relations with the leaders of the centrist movement. I found it quite possible to have the discussions and the negotiations, but, alas, I didn't have the troops to represent. Consequently, it became necessary on my part to cut it out because we had nothing to propose. It is very hard to be a good diplomat when you haven't got an army.

Now, things didn't stand still. Our enemies, as well as our friends, reacted to the intervention of the American party and of Comrade Trotsky and of the Executive Committee of the Fourth International. Our friends reacted not too enthusiastically. But our enemies, the London Bureau, flew into a panic. It appeared to them as a concentration of the Fourth International, which in a way it was. There was the letter of Trotsky to Pivert[67] which was known to all of them. There was a representative of the American party in France. There was the fact that 40 percent of the POI—although they didn't know the percent—had already joined the organization. The London Bureau, which exists only for the purpose of sabotaging the Fourth International, staged a big concentration in France at the same time. I was invited to a discussion at lunch with a group of leading figures of the London Bureau. I, of course, accepted because it is more or less a practice of mine to talk to political opponents. But it is partly, I think, an illustration of the sectarianism of our comrades in France that they don't like to get mixed up in any kind of complications. They had visions of a big betrayal. The truth of the matter was they considered my politics 100 percent centrist to start with. Of course, nothing came of it. It was purely a diplomatic dinner.

I also had some conversations with leaders of the POUM, all of whom converged in Paris after their escape from Barcelona, and all of whom, as was expressed by Comrade Rous, came to Paris to demonstrate that they had not learned anything from their experiences in Spain. I must say it was one of the most depressing afternoons I ever had, the afternoon I talked with Andrade.[68] He is a former member of the International Communist League, was considered the [leader of the] left wing of the POUM. He went through that whole tragic experience. And after we got through talking about the Stalinists and anarchists and other matters, I asked him, "How do you evaluate now the actions of the POUM in signing the program of the People's Front and entering the government of the People's Front?" He said, "I think we did right." There was nothing more to talk about. I felt that it was absolutely useless to talk to these people. They have not learned anything from their experience. The whole bunch of the London Bureau is the same. There is not among them one revolutionary party. The one section of that group that has some vitality—the PSOP—they are trying with might and main to drag into that terrible swamp. And that presents to us and to the workers of France an enormous danger.

These people of the London Bureau specialize in the struggle against us. They devote themselves to weasel attacks in the corner. They shy away from every kind of political discussion. They use every other kind of argument to prove you can't get along with Trotskyites. "Look at the United States—they went into the Socialist Party, they broke it up, and so on." They create an atmosphere where everybody is placed on their guard against our comrades before they begin their work. They are planning for the month of April—right at the

67. Trotsky's letter to Pivert, "Where Is the PSOP Going?," December 22, 1938, and his other writings about the PSOP and Pivert are collected in *Leon Trotsky on France*.

68. Juan Andrade (1897–) was a founder of the Spanish CP, the Spanish Left Opposition, and the POUM, where he was considered a left winger.

present time—another big meeting of their so-called International Front Against War. It seemed to me tragic that at the moment when these people were trying to poison the atmosphere of the PSOP and to set up obstacles and barriers to our penetration that the leaders of our movement complement their work. The London Bureauites work to prevent further entry of our people and to hamper the work of those inside. Our leading comrades did everything they could to accommodate themselves to that policy. The interests of the Fourth International suffered by it.

In addition to that, a new headache developed. You know something about the history of the Molinier faction and the decision of the world congress ratifying the expulsion of M. as an undesirable character. This clique, having completely exhausted the possibility of further maneuvers with our French section, had finally joined the PSOP. They entrenched themselves—about thirty—in the youth organization of the PSOP, and in a short time gained control of it. They claimed they agreed with the Fourth International on everything but, of course, their "methods." They conducted intrigues against us in the ranks. Now, in that situation as it developed, it became more and more clear, not only to me, but to the other members of the Fourth International, that we had to accelerate the actions of our French comrades. They were stewing in their own juices and making no progress whatsoever—standing on one spot. I took part in innumerable meetings. I never had so many discussions, with so many people, over and over again. And always I came out, like Omar Khayyam, the same door wherein I went.

All this time the walls were being built up against our penetration in the PSOP. The "entrist" group headed by Rous was gaining ground, establishing new contacts, having really almost an open door before them, especially until the London Bureauites developed an active policy against us. In a short time they had a debate on Freemasonry, which is a form of chloroforming the class antagonism of the proletariat and is a big issue in France. They had a discussion in Paris with about 1,000 members of the organization in attendance, and the reporter against Freemasonry was one of our comrades. According to the reports I received, a majority of those in attendance, particularly of the workers present, supported the position of our comrades.

Comrades Rous, Craipeau and others were taken into the staff of the official paper and allowed to write articles right away. We were in the American Socialist Party a year, and I think we got only two or three articles in the monthly discussion bulletin. In the Federated Council of Paris, which has delegates from every branch, a number of our comrades were drawn in as delegates right away. Rous was drawn in as a consultative member and given the right to take the floor. Discussions began about the forthcoming convention. Rous announced there that he was going to propose the transitional program of the Fourth International, and Pivert made a motion that he be drawn on to the program commission. Before I left there, Rous had drawn up his statement and had submitted it for discussion in mimeographed form throughout the organization. Comrade Craipeau organized in the space of a month two or three new branches in the neighborhood he worked.

In general, I cite all these facts to show that the general atmosphere of the PSOP was favorable to the intervention of our comrades and the possibility of their working. Rous wrote a pamphlet on the Spanish catastrophe which is sold through party channels, as well as by our group.

A week or so before I left they came out with a monthly magazine almost as large as the *New International*, published by Rous, full of Bolshevik articles. While they were doing this, the POI was not able to record any progress whatsoever. We began to press the leading comrades at least for the entry of the youth of the Fourth International into the PSOP to chase away those Molinier usurpers and give the youth a revolutionary direction. And then, finally, we had to conclude that there was absolutely no political way out in the next period except a complete entry into the PSOP. We began to press for an entry both of the adult organization and of the youth. The result of the pressure was that a majority of the Executive Committee of the youth pronounced itself in favor of the entry but did not have a majority of the rank and file. A strong minority of the POI took a position in favor of entry, but were not able, at least in the immediate situation, to swing the whole thing around.

I don't know how that will impress you—whether that is due to incompetence on my part or whether it was a task that could not be solved at one stroke—I don't know. It is possible that the task might have been accomplished more successfully and more cleverly by someone else. My opinion is that the problem was so deeply rooted in political differences that it was utopian to think that it could be done with one stroke. When you recall our own experience—how long it took us to transform the Workers Party from a majority of opposition to any kind of maneuvers with the Socialist Party to a position where the party would be ready to enter the Socialist Party when the situation became ripe, that it involved at least a solid year of a very sharp and protracted faction fight and even a split, that the fight was conducted by a strong group of the party, when you recall this, you realize that such transformations, such victories over sectarianism, are not to be solved overnight.

Then I, of course, had additional handicaps. The fact that I was a foreigner and had language difficulties, and that it was necessary for me to work with the greatest caution, that I could not afford to go to membership meetings, and the fact that I never had any cooperation from the leaders—and I was compelled to work entirely through the leaders—you can see it wasn't exactly an easy task.

In my opinion, now after thinking of the thing from a distance since my departure, the solution of the problem in France cannot come by top negotiations with the leadership. All the diplomacy and cleverness in the world will not solve the problem, which is that of smashing sectarianism. And that can only be done by an appeal to the rank and file of the organization. And this became more and more the opinion of the Executive Committee of the Fourth International.

A short time before I left, we held another meeting of the Executive Committee of the Fourth International. We had representatives from Poland, from Greece, from France, from the U.S., from England and Belgium. At this meeting, after prolonged discussion, the entire Executive Committee, the Belgian, the English, Polish, American, and one other, I can't recall at the moment, excluding the French, voted to recommend again to the POI to enter the PSOP and emphasized its recommendation that the youth join immediately and without conditions.

When that brought no results, when the comrades were not disposed to yield to that third intervention of the Executive Committee, it seemed to me that we had come to a stalemate and that it would be unprofitable for me to work there under those conditions until our National Committee had given the matter further consideration. It seemed necessary for me to return home for consultation with the NC—not about an abandonment of the struggle, but about a new form and method of conducting it.

We have had this matter up for discussion in the NC. We have taken decisions to continue our intervention to maintain a representative in France and to continue to assist in every way we can. That is the way the matter now stands. I think we can be reasonably optimistic that in the next few months we will succeed in solving the problem. I am sure that the position of the committee will be supported by Comrade Trotsky also. Our [National] Committee voted unanimously to endorse the decision of the Executive Committee of the Fourth International in recommending entry into the PSOP.

The general conclusion as I see it is that the problem of the French section remains for us a problem of tremendous importance that is not diminished by the difficulties that we have encountered. We have to recognize that our attempt to solve the problem at one stroke has not met with success. That is not our fault, and we need not be discouraged about it. It only means we must try a new means of attack. We have to tackle the problem from a new angle and try to solve it by stages.

In any case, a continuous intervention in France is an absolute necessity for us. It is necessary for us to maintain a representative in France, to issue an appeal to their ranks in a form which will be best calculated to get a response from them.

Whatever the result may be, we are the gainers for the effort we have made. We have not only helped already—and that is testified to in more ways than one by the group of Fourth Internationalists in the PSOP—but we have also learned something from it. We have the satisfaction that we once again transformed our internationalism from words into deed. That in itself is a great step forward for our party.

SELECTED TITLES BY JAMES P. CANNON

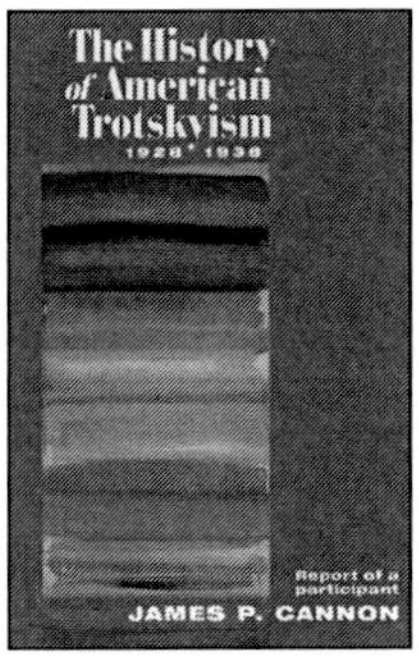

The History of American Trotskyism, 1928–1938

Report of a Participant

"Trotskyism is not a new movement, a new doctrine," Cannon says, "but the restoration, the revival of genuine Marxism as it was expounded and practiced in the Russian revolution and in the early days of the Communist International." In twelve talks given in 1942, Cannon recounts a decisive period in efforts to build a proletarian party in the United States. $22. Also in Spanish and French.

The Struggle for a Proletarian Party

"The workers of America have power enough to topple the structure of capitalism at home and to lift the whole world with them when they rise," Cannon asserts. On the eve of World War II, a founder of the communist movement in the US and leader of the Communist International in Lenin's time defends the program and party-building norms of Bolshevism. $22

Speeches to the Party

The Revolutionary Perspective and the Revolutionary Party

Writing in the early 1950s, Cannon discusses how class-conscious workers, in face of the conservatizing pressures of the emerging capitalist expansion and anticommunist witch-hunt, carried out effective union work and political activity to build a communist workers party. He discusses Washington's failure to achieve its goals in the Korean War and why the rulers reined in McCarthyism. $24

The First Ten Years of American Communism

Report of a Participant

"Stalinism has worked mightily to obliterate the honorable record of American communism in its pioneer days. Yet the Communist Party wrote such a chapter too, and the young militants of the new generation ought to know about it and claim it for their own. It belongs to them."—James P. Cannon, 1962. $22

The Socialist Workers Party in World War II

Writings and Speeches, 1940–1943

Preparing the communist workers movement in the United States to campaign against wartime censorship, repression, and antiunion assaults. $25

The Struggle for Socialism in the 'American Century'

Writings and Speeches, 1945–1947

The challenges posed by the post–World War II labor upsurge, the rapid expansion of openings for the communist movement, and the subsequent ebb in face of the stabilization of US capitalism and the employers' antilabor offensive and witch-hunt. $25

NEW FROM PATHFINDER

The Cuban Five

Who They Are
Why They Were Framed
Why They Should Be Free

Presents the facts on the worldwide struggle to free Gerardo Hernández, Ramón Labañino, Antonio Guerrero, Fernando González, and René González. Shows how this battle to defend the Five is part of the class struggle in the US, where millions of working people know how the courts and prisons are used to punish those who refuse to accept the conditions imposed on us by capitalism. $5. Also in Spanish and French.

Cuba and Angola

Fighting for Africa's Freedom and Our Own

The story of Cuba's nearly 16-year internationalist mission to aid the people of Angola, in the words of those who made that history, including Fidel Castro, Nelson Mandela, and Raúl Castro. With a special feature by Gabriel García Márquez. Also includes accounts by three of the Cuban Five who fought in Angola. $12. Also in Spanish.

"I will die the way I've lived"

15 watercolors by Antonio Guerrero on the 15th anniversary of the imprisonment of the Cuban Five

Fifteen paintings that graphically portray the 17 months the Cuban Five spent in the "hole" at the Federal Detention Center in Miami following their arrest in 1998. A window through which workers everywhere can identify with the battles waged by the Five and appreciate not only their integrity, courage, and creativity but also their sense of humor. $7. Also in Spanish and French.

Voices from Prison

The Cuban Five

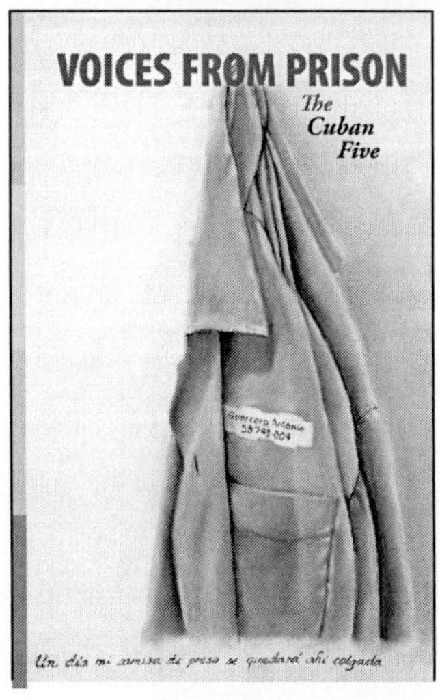

The revolutionary integrity, strength, and humanity of the Five come through in the voices heard here. Above all, we see the respect they have won for themselves among other prisoners. And why the same happens among working people everywhere who have experienced in their own lives the effects of capitalist "justice." $7. Also in Spanish, French, and Arabic.

EXPAND YOUR REVOLUTIONARY LIBRARY

50 Years of Covert Operations in the US

Washington's political police and the American working class

LARRY SEIGLE, FARRELL DOBBS, STEVE CLARK

The 15-year political campaign of the Socialist Workers Party to expose decades of spying and disruption by the FBI and other federal cop agencies targeting working-class organizations and other opponents of government policies. Traces the origins of bipartisan efforts to expand presidential powers and build the "national security" state essential to maintaining capitalist rule. Includes "Imperialist War and the Working Class" by Farrell Dobbs. $12. Also in Spanish.

Socialism on Trial

Testimony at Minneapolis Sedition Trial

JAMES P. CANNON

The revolutionary program of the working class, as presented during the 1941 trial of leaders of the Minneapolis labor movement and the Socialist Workers Party for "seditious conspiracy." Includes Cannon's answer to ultraleft critics of the defendants, drawing lessons from the working-class movement from Marx and Engels to the October 1917 revolution in Russia and beyond. $16. Also in Spanish.

Women in Cuba: The Making of a Revolution Within the Revolution

From Santiago de Cuba and the Rebel Army, to the Birth of the Federation of Cuban Women

VILMA ESPÍN, ASELA DE LOS SANTOS, YOLANDA FERRER

The social revolution that in 1959 brought down the bloody Batista dictatorship began in the streets of cities like Santiago de Cuba and the Rebel Army's liberated mountain zones of eastern Cuba. The unprecedented integration of women in the ranks and leadership of this struggle was a true measure of the revolutionary course it has followed to this day. Here, in firsthand accounts by women who helped make it, is the story of that revolution—and "the revolution within." Introduction by Mary-Alice Waters. $20. Also in Spanish.

Lenin's Final Fight

Speeches and Writings, 1922–23

V.I. LENIN

In 1922 and 1923, V.I. Lenin, central leader of the world's first socialist revolution, waged what was to be his last political battle. At stake was whether that revolution, and the international movement it led, would remain on the proletarian course that had brought workers and peasants to power in October 1917. Indispensable to understanding how the privileged caste led by Stalin arose and the consequences for the class struggle in the 20th and 21st centuries. $20. Also in Spanish.

New International

A MAGAZINE OF MARXIST POLITICS AND THEORY

REVOLUTION, INTERNATIONALISM, AND SOCIALISM: THE LAST YEAR OF MALCOLM X

JACK BARNES

In addition to the lead article, "The Last Year of Malcolm X," this issue contains "The Clintons' Antilabor Legacy: Roots of the 2008 World Financial Crisis." Jack Barnes explains how the Clinton administration, and both Republican and Democratic administrations before it, stepped up assaults on working people and, at the same time, helped bring on the massive mortgage, household, corporate, and government debts that are by-products of today's world crisis of capitalist production. The results for workers and farmers worldwide are devastating. *Also in No. 14:* "The Stewardship of Nature Also Falls to the Working Class"; *and* "Setting the Record Straight on Fascism and World War II." $14. Also in Spanish, French, and Swedish.

CAPITALISM'S LONG HOT WINTER HAS BEGUN

JACK BARNES

Today's accelerating global capitalist crisis—the opening stages of what will be decades of economic, financial, and social convulsions and class battles—accompanies a continuation of the most far-reaching shift in Washington's military policy and organization since the US buildup toward World War II. Class-struggle-minded working people must face this historic turning point for imperialism, and draw satisfaction from being "in their face" as we chart a revolutionary course to confront it. In *New International* no. 12. $16. Also in Spanish, French, Swedish, and Arabic.

OUR POLITICS START WITH THE WORLD

In *New International* no. 13. $14. Also in Spanish, French, and Swedish.

THE FIGHT FOR A WORKERS AND FARMERS GOVERNMENT IN THE U.S.

In *New International* no. 4. $14

From the Escambray to the Congo

In the Whirlwind of the Cuban Revolution

VÍCTOR DREKE

The author describes how easy it became after the Cuban Revolution to take down a rope segregating blacks from whites in the town square, yet how enormous was the battle to transform social relations underlying all the "ropes" inherited from capitalism and Yankee domination. Dreke, second in command of the internationalist column in the Congo led by Che Guevara in 1965, recounts the creative joy with which working people have defended their revolutionary course—from Cuba's Escambray mountains to Africa and beyond. $18. Also in Spanish.

The Jewish Question

A Marxist Interpretation

ABRAM LEON

Traces the historical rationalizations of anti-Semitism to the fact that, in the centuries preceding the domination of industrial capitalism, Jews emerged as a "people-class" of merchants, moneylenders, and traders. Leon explains why the propertied rulers incite renewed Jew-hatred in the epoch of capitalism's decline. $22

The Working Class and the Transformation of Learning

The Fraud of Education Reform under Capitalism

JACK BARNES

"Until society is reorganized so that education is a human activity from the time we are very young until the time we die, there will be no education worthy of working, creating humanity." $3. Also in Spanish, French, Swedish, Icelandic, Farsi, and Greek.

February 1965: The Final Speeches

MALCOLM X

Speeches from the last three weeks of the life of this outstanding leader of the oppressed Black nationality and of the working class in the United States. A large part is material previously unavailable, with some in print for the first time. $19

The Communist Manifesto

KARL MARX, FREDERICK ENGELS

Why communism is not a set of preconceived principles but the line of march of the working class toward power, "springing from an existing class struggle, a historical movement going on under our very eyes." The founding document of the modern revolutionary workers movement. $5. Also in Spanish, French, and Arabic.

Socialism: Utopian and Scientific

FREDERICK ENGELS

"To make man the master of his own form of social organization—to make him free—is the historical mission of the modern proletariat," writes Engels. Here socialism is placed on a scientific foundation, the product of the lawful operations of capitalism itself and the struggles of the working class. $12

Thomas Sankara Speaks

The Burkina Faso Revolution, 1983–87

Under Sankara's leadership, the revolutionary government of Burkina Faso in West Africa set an electrifying example. Peasants, workers, women, and youth mobilized to carry out literacy and immunization drives; to sink wells, plant trees, build dams, erect housing; to combat the oppression of women and transform exploitative relations on the land; to free themselves from the imperialist yoke and solidarize with others engaged in that fight internationally. $24. Also in French.

Abortion Is a Woman's Right!

PAT GROGAN, EVELYN REED

Why abortion rights are central not only to the fight for the full emancipation of women, but to forging a united and fighting labor movement. $6. Also in Spanish.

Cosmetics, Fashions, and the Exploitation of Women

JOSEPH HANSEN, EVELYN REED, MARY-ALICE WATERS

Sixty years ago, an article published in the socialist weekly the *Militant* sparked a lively debate on how the cosmetics and "fashion" industries play on the economic and emotional insecurities of women and youth to rake in profits. Today that exchange, contained in this book, a Marxist classic, offers an introduction to the origin of women's oppression and the struggle for liberation. $15. Also in Spanish.

Che Guevara Talks to Young People

The Argentine-born revolutionary leader challenges youth of Cuba and the world to study, to work, to become disciplined. To join the front lines of struggles, small and large. To politicize themselves and the work of their organizations. To become a different kind of human being as they strive with working people of all lands to transform the world. Eight talks from 1959 to 1964. $15. Also in Spanish.

Teamster Rebellion

FARRELL DOBBS

The 1934 strikes that built the industrial union movement in Minneapolis and helped pave the way for the CIO, recounted by a central leader of that battle. The first of four volumes on the strikes and organizing drives that transformed the Teamsters union in the Midwest into a fighting social movement and pointed the road toward independent labor political action. $19. Also in Spanish, French, and Swedish.

Education for Socialists Series

The Workers and Farmers Government
by Joseph Hansen. $10

For a Workers and Farmers Government in the United States
by Jack Barnes. $10

The Nicaraguan Workers and Farmers Government
by Jack Barnes. $6

Marxism and the Working Farmer
by Doug Jenness, with documents and speeches by Frederick Engels, V.I. Lenin, and Fidel Castro. $12

Proletarian Leadership in Power
What We Can Learn from Lenin, Castro, and the FSLN
by Mary-Alice Waters. $6

Grenada: A Workers and Farmers Government
by Steve Clark. $6

Class, Party, and State, and the Eastern European Revolution. $7

The Chinese Revolution and Its Development. $8

Maoism vs. Bolshevism
The 1965 Catastrophe in Indonesia, China's "Cultural Revolution," and the Disintegration of World Stalinism
by Joseph Hansen. $12

Workers and Farmers Governments since the Second World War
by Robert Chester. $6

The Organizational Character of the Socialist Workers Party
1965 resolution of the SWP. $5

The Structure and Organizational Principles of the Party
by Farrell Dobbs. $6

Background to "The Changing Face of U.S. Politics" and "U.S. Imperialism Has Lost the Cold War"
by Jack Barnes, et al. $7

Background to "The Struggle for a Proletarian Party"
Articles by Leon Trotsky and James P. Cannon. $7

In Defense of Revolutionary Centralism
by Jack Barnes. $5

1999 Preface to "The Changing Face of U.S. Politics"
by Mary-Alice Waters. $4

The Abern Clique
by Joseph Hansen. $6

The Revolutionary Perspective for the United States
Theses on the American Revolution
by James P. Cannon. $6

Aspects of Socialist Election Policy
edited by Doug Jenness. $10

James P. Cannon: A Political Tribute
Including five interviews from the last year of his life. $8.50

James P. Cannon: The Internationalist
by Joseph Hansen, appendices by James P. Cannon. $8

Countermobilization: A Strategy to Fight Racist and Fascist Attacks
by Farrell Dobbs. $8

The Fight against Fascism in the U.S.A.
Forty Years of Struggle Described by Participants
by James P. Cannon, et al. $8

What Is American Fascism?
Writings on Father Coughlin, Mayor Frank Hague, and Sen. Joseph McCarthy
by James P. Cannon and Joseph Hansen. $8

From Mississippi to Boston
The Demand for Troops to Enforce Civil Rights. $6

Selected Speeches of Fidel Castro. $15

Fidel Castro on Chile. $20

Revolutionary Cuba Today
The Record of a Debate by Larry Seigle, et al. $12

Bolshevism and the Russian Revolution: A Debate
by Doug Jenness and Ernest Mandel. $12

Two Study Guides on Lenin's Writings
by Steve Clark and John Riddell. $5

Study Guide to "Lenin's Struggle for a Revolutionary International." $5

Communist Continuity and the Fight for Women's Liberation
Documents of the Socialist Workers Party, 1971–86
Edited by Mary-Alice Waters. 3-volume set, $30
Women's Liberation and the Line of March of the Working Class (Part I). $12
Women, Leadership, and the Proletarian Norms of the Communist Movement (Part II). $12
Abortion Rights, the ERA, and the Rebirth of a Feminist Movement (Part III). $12

Independent Black Political Action (1954–78)
The Struggle to Break with the Democratic and Republican Parties
by Mac Warren. $8

The National Black Independent Political Party
An Important Step Forward for Blacks and Other American Workers
by Nan Bailey, et al. $5

Selected Articles on the Labor Movement (Recent Trends)
by Farrell Dobbs. $5

Selected Documents on SWP Trade Union Policy (1972). $5

Class Struggle Policy in the Rise of the Labor Movement
by Tom Kerry. $5

Defense Policies and Principles of the Socialist Workers Party
by George Novack. $5

Against Violence within the Workers Movement. $5

Revolutionary Strategy in the Fight against the Vietnam War
by James P. Cannon, Farrell Dobbs, Jack Barnes, et al. $13

Israel and the Arab Revolution
by Gus Horowitz. $10

Towards a History of the Fourth International
16-volume set, $95
(Individual volumes available, write for listing and prices.)

The Development and Disintegration of World Stalinism. $9

Healy's Big Lie
The Slander Campaign against Joseph Hansen and George Novack
by Joseph Hansen, et al. $10

Marxism versus Ultraleftism
The Record of Healy's Break with Marxism
edited by Joseph Hansen. $15